10. 52

Y1.99

Heather in my Ears

Angus MacVicar

Heather in my Ears

MORE CONFESSIONS OF
A MINISTER'S SON

HUTCHINSON OF LONDON

Hutchinson & Co (Publishers) Ltd
3 Fitzroy Square, London W1

An imprint of the Hutchinson Publishing Group

London Melbourne Sydney Auckland
Wellington Johannesburg Cape Town
and agencies throughout the world

First published March 1974
Second impression November 1974
© Angus MacVicar 1974

Printed in Great Britain by litho by The Anchor Press Ltd
and bound by Wm Brendon & Son Ltd
both of Tiptree, Essex

ISBN 0 09 119020 7

To Jean and Jock
who bravely bear with me

Acknowledgements

For permission to reproduce photographs my grateful thanks are due to the Rev. Ronald Falconer, DD; Dr R. N. M. MacSween; Mr W. J. Anderson, MBE, and Mr Gordon Hunter. Copyright in the pictures of Southend Parish Church and St. Columba's Footsteps belongs to the Royal Commission on the Ancient and Historical Monuments of Scotland, to whom I am greatly indebted for allowing me to use them.

A.M.

Contents

Illustrations

In the Vaward of our Youth

The old Manse has had a face-lift. The Virginia creeper above the front door has gone, cut down to facilitate new harling. The sloping lawn, bordered with concrete and no longer unkempt, is pastel green evidence of muscular mowing and rolling. Replacing fires of coal and logs, a central heating plant now roars and bubbles in what we used to call 'the paraffin house'.

When we were children the Manse was surrounded by trees, one of them a magnificent copper beech with a swing hanging from a lower branch. On a winter's night, half a century ago, my two older brothers and I used to cower in our beds in the room above the kitchen and listen to the wind soughing through their branches. It was a strange sound, inexplicably sad.

Once, years later, I lay awake in the same bedroom listening to the same sound. In the morning, at the cold, raw hour of six o'clock, I was leaving the Manse, perhaps for good. The early steamer from Campbeltown, the old *Davaar*, would take me to Gourock, from where a clattering train would spew me out into the streets of Glasgow towards the imponderable dangers of the University. The sound in the trees made me want to cry, and I knew at last what it meant for me: the repeating heart-sigh of humanity for things that will never be again.

But when we were small the sound was merely frightening. As the eldest, I made up stories about the trees to comfort Archie and Willie—and myself. They were friendly giants, I would tell them, on sentry duty around the Manse to guard the people inside. The sound was their way of talking, of assuring us that no ghosts or ghoulies would get near the house if they could help it.

Hypocrisy, perhaps, has always been my middle name. As

Archie and Willie grew older and the second half of the family, Rona Kenneth and John, began to join us, I instituted what I called 'a test of manhood' for MacVicar males. (Rona, being a girl and therefore somehow sacred, was exempt.) When, one after another they reached the age of about five or six, I would wait for a peat-black night in which the trees moaned even louder than usual. Then I'd dare them to climb the creaking wooden stairs to the empty attics and remain up there for five minutes, in the dark and alone. No lamps or candles were allowed; and, of course, there was no electric light.

As the youngest, John was last to 'thole' the test. By then I was working as a reporter on the *Campbeltown Courier*, Archie was studying English at Glasgow University and Willie was an apprentice seaman. As it happened, however, we were all at home to witness the traditional ceremony, on this occasion arranged by Rona and Kenneth, still at school.

Aged only four, John was a small, round-faced boy with silky hair the colour of bleached straw. He stood at the bottom of the stairs, contemplating the cold darkness above and trying not to show how terrified he was.

He looked back at Rona and Kenneth. They were very young, not yet capable of compassion. He looked at the rest of us and saw no sympathy in our faces either. Archie and Willie were men of the world, and so, I believed, was I. The test had to proceed, for the sake of John's own character.

'Get a move on,' said Kenneth.

'You'll be a man when you come down,' said Rona. 'Think of that.'

Archie and Willie, harbouring vague guilt, tried to reassure him, making disparaging remarks about those who fondly believed in ghosts.

The big trees outside huffed and puffed and ground their teeth. Wind shrieked in an ill-fitting skylight in one of the attics. John's lips trembled.

From a lofty, philosophical height I smiled down and patted his head. 'Face this and you'll face anything', I said. 'It's for your own good.'

Unwillingly he turned away from us, hope gone, and began to climb the stairs. His back was hunched. Short, fat legs found tall steps difficult. He faltered as he came to the bend and faced the utter darkness higher up. Then the small legs began moving again, and he disappeared. We heard him reach the attic landing. There was a shuffling sound, followed by a wind-scarred silence.

Seconds passed. We shifted about, uneasily.

'Has he fainted?' Rona whispered.

'Maybe he's dead,' said Kenneth.

Archie and Willie looked at me, expecting leadership.

Still no sound from John. A faint tapping occurred on the roof of the Manse. Logic told me it came from the branch of a tree, bending and whipping in the wind. Imagination limned a picture of John's soul struggling to break through the roof and escape to heaven.

I shouted up: 'Okay, I'm coming for you.'

I had a battery torch, a prized Christmas present from my girl-friend, Jean. I switched it on and went clattering up the stairs. In its beam I saw him on the landing, rising from his knees.

'What were you doing?' I said.

'Saying my prayers to myself: "Gentle Jesus, meek and mild . . ."'

'Well, it's all over. Come on down.'

He took my hand. 'Am I a man now?'

'You certainly are.'

We rejoined the others at the foot of the stairs. John received congratulations from them all and for the rest of the evening was so stuffed with pride that he became obnoxious. It's a way the MacVicars have: vicious in defeat, insufferable in victory.

Willie is now senior skipper with the Anchor Line. Kenneth is minister of Kenmore in Perthshire. John himself is Professor of Midwifery at Leicester University. At times of crisis I think they all say their prayers—as I do—and try to stick it out, sometimes with success, sometimes without.

Archie and Rona became teachers. Commanding a platoon of Argylls, Archie died at Gerbini in Sicily in 1943, struck by bullets from a German machine gun. Rona died of cancer in 1949, less than a year after joyfully singing her way to a gold medal at the

National Mod in Glasgow. I often wonder if in their last crises they heard the wind in the Manse trees and found comfort in prayer. I hope they did.

But most of the trees are now gone. Maimie, our old maid, died first, then my mother, then my father at the age of 92. In 1963, when my mother left us, the copper beech had begun to wither, and the swing, maintained for the use of children in the parish, was cut down, because the branch which supported it had become unsafe. In 1970, the year my father died, the lovely tree itself was destroyed, along with a dozen others.

I was happy to see them go, so that light and air would greet our new young minister and his wife and boys. The world doesn't stop because a person dies or a tree is felled. You have memories, and they are happy. And after all, it's on good memories that the future is built.

My father and mother were both young when they came to the Manse of Southend, Kintyre, in 1910. So was I, only eighteen months. And so was Jessie MacLaren, the maid, whom we later called Maimie and whom we all loved, in spite of her sharp tongue and knuckly, punishing hands.

Though I don't remember it—I'd have to be another Compton MacKenzie to do that—the 'flitting' from Duror in Appin must have been an exciting adventure, with my mother and Maimie doing most of the planning and all the hard work, and my father dodging the column as usual but encouraging his women-folk by unctuously repeating the family motto, *Dominus providebit* ('The Lord will provide').

When Archie arrived in 1912, he was the first baby to be born in the Manse for over 70 years. Three previous ministers had been either bachelors or childless. My father and mother proceeded to make up for lost time and called a halt only when John was born in 1927.

The main block of the Manse was built in 1818, additions and improvements being made in 1881. The result is a house with two big public rooms, six bedrooms (including two attics) a large kitchen, a scullery and two bathrooms. Along with a number of outhouses, relics of an era when ministers were also farmers and made pocket-money out of cultivating the glebe, it stands near the church in about two acres of ground.

For children growing up it was an ideal place, and we made full use of all the nooks and crannies inside and of the cowboy and Indian territory, covered with grass, trees and shrubs, which lay out of doors. Platoons of other children used to join us, scarring the attic wallpaper in wild winter ploys and trampling through my father's vegetable plots in the summer time.

When we played in the garden, creating damage, and he came after us in righteous rage, we hid under the gooseberry bushes or between the rows of green peas, containing hunger by picking and eating the produce so fortunately to hand.

There is danger, of course, when children run amok in open spaces. Archie had his forehead split open when essaying a trapeze dive from the swing. Scrabbling through the undergrowth in the back garden, looking for a lost ball, Willie cut the base of his thumb on a broken bottle—with a startling loss of blood— and bears the scar to this day. On separate occasions I sprained both arms falling from trees and now, as a probable result, suffer from rheumatism in the elbows. (A fine excuse, at times, for erratic performances at the golf.)

Quite often, encouraged by my mother and Maimie, both of whom must have longed for peace, my father would take us with him on a round of parish visits. Some of these we didn't enjoy, because the people would act 'holy' in the presence of the minister and so appear to us uninteresting. Others we looked forward to with pleasure.

One such was to a farm cottage where an old lady lived alone —alone, that is, except for a cockatoo which could talk. Not only talk: it could swear with an enthusiasm which today would out-Warhol Warhol. Under the friendly scrutiny of old Maggie, we'd stand beneath the cage, whistling and cajoling, trying to make it reply. When it did, with fearful oaths, we would squirm with delight, always, however, keeping a careful eye on our father to see how he was taking it. But Maggie, with her own bawdily

cheerful conversation usually kept him laughing and in a tolerant
mood.

She was old, bent from toil on the farms, but to us she seemed
remarkably happy, with her memories and her cockatoo. I believe
the cockatoo was a present from an old 'lad', who'd been a sailor.
We thought it incredible that Maggie could ever have had a 'lad'.
But her easy way of talking to children and her quick, infectious
laughter should have given us a clue.

Another place we liked to visit was a remote sheep farm occupied
by Archie Campbell, with his cousin Rosie and brother Ned. Archie
had a white beard and was, for a time, chairman of Southend
Parish Council. His wit was as clear—and as kindly— as the
sunshine on Glenbreckrie, where for years he tramped the heathery
braes as a shepherd. He was descended from the MacNeills,
an aristocratic family in Kintyre, and, as my mother used to say,
'the mark of the gentleman was on him'. He spoke straightly and
honestly, but never, if he could help it, did he say anything to
hurt.

We were fascinated by the decor in his sitting-room. The walls
were covered with fuzzy, enlarged photographs of prize-winning
sheep, all looking towards the camera like smug beauty queens.
Purple plush, with dangling bobbles, swathed the mantelpiece,
above which hung a reproduction of *The Stag at Bay*. On the side-
board numerous silver frames contained pictures of ancient
MacNeills and Campbells.

The fire in the wide iron grate was of peat. Its aroma was temp-
ered by the flavour of butter, cheese and milk from the nearby
dairy.

Old Archie's hospitality was unfailing. When my father called,
one of the first objects to appear on the table was a bottle of
whisky. If we were with him, a jug of milk would also be brought
in by Rosie, the lady of the house.   One day, this ritual having
been observed, Archie, said: 'And now, minister, after your
long walk, will you be having a dram?'

'Thank you, Archie.'

'And you, Angus?'—pointing to me, aged ten.

'A glass of milk, please.'

'And Archie?'—indicating my brother, aged seven.

'A glass of milk, please.'

Then to Willie, aged five: 'And what about yourself, *laochain*? Tell me what you'd like.'

As usual sparing of words, the master mariner of a time to come said nothing. He merely pointed at the whisky bottle.

Archie's face broke into a happy smile. 'Ah!' he said, patting my brother's head. 'There's a great future in front of you, my boy!'

A wooden bridge, with a handrail on one side only, led over the Breckrie burn into the garden of Archie's house. Beside the bridge there used to stand two rowan trees.

Once, on our way home from a visit to the Campbells, we sat down to rest on an old turf dyke. The glen below was bursting into green. Tightly curled leaves were spiking out of sticky sheaths on sycamores and birches. Grass was showing among the heather on the opposite hillside and, beside the road, wild hyacinth shoots were beginning to thrust upwards. Blackbirds and thrushes, some courting, provided a treble accompaniment to the continuous bass of the quick-running burn. Everywhere was the scent of spring, acrid and earthy, the very scent of life itself.

The turf dyke on which we sat, my father told us, had once enclosed a croft-house, and, indeed, we could still see traces of a moss-grown ruin. At an opening in the dyke stood a mountain ash, which, in Scotland, is called a rowan.

Always curious, Archie asked why rowans should so often be found near the front door of a house.

'It was considered lucky,' my father said. 'I knew an old lady in Inverness-shire, when I was a student missionary there, who always had rowan twigs in the kitchen. For peace and prosperity she said. Her husband was a crofter, who sometimes fished in Loch Ness. He would stick pieces of rowan wood in the thatch above the byre door, and I've seen him put a wreath of rowan berries on the bow of his boat.'

'To ward off the evil eye?' I said.

'Of course. There was another old lady in Islay, where I spent a summer preaching, who put crosses of rowan twigs below her milk basins. If she didn't the milk turned sour. Or so she told me.'

I was to discover rowan trees by many another ruined gate and to become acquainted with books, like *The Golden Bough*, which referred to the Druidical worship of the rowan—or, rather, of the spirit of a dead person within the rowan. I was to come to the conclusion, as my father did, that pagan race memories take 'an unconscionable time a-dying'.

Archie and Willie and I, approaching adolescence, were press-ganged into doing spade-work in the vegetable garden, under a paternal eye. In our stead Rona and Kenneth and John continued to play happily on the lawn in front of the Manse. At one stage they were joined by Rob, the sealyham, a cunning player of hide-and-seek. His use of cover, particularly in the big rhododendron copse, was remarkable.

I'll swear, too, that he had a sense of humour. One day, as Kenneth pursued John across the lawn and was about to over-take him, Rob dashed in front and deliberately tripped him up. There was a triumphant barking, followed by much affectionate face-licking as Kenneth got ruefully to his feet.

Rob, as one of the household, loved us all impartially. His pedigree was distinguished, but we never thought of showing him. He was a friend, and you don't inconvenience or exploit a friend to boost your own ego.

For a number of years he was happy at the Manse, until a tragedy occurred. Ewes and lambs were being worried in nearby fields, and somebody said he'd seen the Manse dog close to the scene of one of the killings. We knew it wasn't true, but the law of the countryside is harsh and Rob had to go. Soon afterwards a brown collie belonging to the informer was found to be the real culprit.

There was no successor to Rob. It's a paradox that the country-side is no place for a pet dog, unless you're prepared to give it exercise on a leash. When sheep are being worried a roaming pet is always the first to be accused. And, anyway, life on a leash is never happy either for a dog or for a man.

Rob was presented to us by the shooters, a family group of sportsmen who rented moors and rivers in Southend from the

Duke of Argyll. They stayed at the inn, usually from August to October. During the day they tramped the moors, accompanied by gamekeeper and ghillies, string bags bulging with feather and fur. In the evening, by lamplight, they sat down to their meal in dinner-jackets and dinner-gowns.

To us, peering from outside through the windows of the inn this was a great wonder. Most of the farming folk in my father's congregation could afford neither a holiday nor fancy clothes simply for eating in. The few who did have money in the bank were disinclined, temperamentally, to squander it.

In Southend, at the beginning of the century, status was won not by parading leisure and expensive garments but by a show of hard physical work from dawn to dusk each day.

For males the badges of rectitude were thick cloth caps, sometimes worn back to front in a high wind, collarless blue blouses called (phonetically) 'carsekies', and hodden grey trousers tied below the knee with leather straps or pieces of twine called (again phonetically) 'booyangs'. Heavy tackety boots, mud-stained for preference, were also *de rigueur*.

Some of the older farmers didn't work all that hard, but they saw to it that their families and their servants did. Skilfully, they themselves gave the impression of being constantly busy, even though their hard day's darg often brought them to the 'smiddy' for a gossip with Ned MacCallum, the blacksmith, who conducted a local Exchange Telegraph and Central News, or to the inn for a warming pick-me-up before the mid-day meal.

The ladies, young and old, wore dull, ankle-length dresses of thick material. Any splash of colour marked the wearer as a 'flighty piece'. Or—the ultimate sin—a 'lazy bitch'. They milked the cows by hand and laboured at the manufacture of butter and cheese. They scrubbed dairies, looked after the cooking, mending and other household work, bore a child every second year and grew old and bent before their time. An hour in church on Sunday and an occasional drive in a horse-drawn machine for shopping in Campbeltown, ten miles away, comprised the only time off they ever got. They were the real workers, not the men—an echo, perhaps, of tribal days when women cultivated the crofts and men played at being fighting warriors.

Farm servants found it difficult to make ends meet. No wonder, when a head ploughman was considered well off with £18 in a half year. Of course, if single, they slept in the farmhouse and got most of their meals there. If married, they had the use of dark, insanitary cottages and occasional perks such as potatoes, butter and milk. Sometimes a married woman would be lucky enough to get a milking job at the farm (twice daily, including Sundays) at half-a-crown a week.

Their leisure hours were few; but when they did have time off, in the evenings, they had no radio or television, no cinema, no discotheque. Encouraged by the Kirk Session, the Dowager Duchess of Argyll built a hall in the Manse grounds in 1911. She filled it with books and games, and my father made it the headquarters of a Young Men's Guild. The hall was used by many in the parish, but in those days, when farmers and their 'fee'd men' mixed uneasily in a social context, only a few farm servants took advantage of the facilities. Instead they tended to congregate at accustomed places, like, for example, the Mill Road End, a wide junction near the Manse, where they held impromptu concerts and dances. I remember on many a summer night, after going to bed, listening to the music of the concertinas, a background to shrieks from the girls and 'hooching' by the men.

Young male farm servants were proud of their physical strength. Occasionally, when the weather was bad, they met in some empty barn to test their prowess. Often, as a small boy, I stood amazed as a sturdy character called John Park lifted two fifty-six pound weights above his head, one suspended on each pinkie. Another ploy was to make two husky lads sit on the floor facing each other, legs straight, the soles of their boots tight together. Leaning forward they gripped the handle of a hoe or hayrake and then, on a signal, heaved back. The winner was the one whose mighty muscles raised his opponent's bottom off the floor.

Some young people today, for whom every kind of recreational activity is provided, practise vandalism and wanton destruction on a depressing scale. Compared with them the farm servants of fifty years ago, whose welfare was considered only by the church and a few enlightened laymen, were models of propriety. But at times they carried out practical jokes which betrayed humour rather than delinquency.

There was an old farmer in Southend, a bachelor, who mocked so loudly at tales of ghosts and poltergeists that he was clearly afraid of them. A number of young farm servants—one of them his own ploughman—decided to test his mettle. On a Hallowe'en night, while he snored in his upstairs bedroom, they took the wheels off a cart in the yard outside, manoeuvred it sideways into the kitchen and then put on the wheels again. When, in the morning, the old farmer made a sleepy way downstairs and saw the huge cart filling his kitchen, its trams reaching for the ceiling, he almost had a stroke. He rushed off to the Manse to confess his sins and took a lot of convincing that the 'happening' must surely have been arranged by practical jokers.

Half a century ago the only country holidays were the Fast Days in June and December and the Fair Days at Candlemass, Whitsunday, Lammas and Martinmass.

The Fast Days, occurring on the Thursday preceding a communion, are relics of a stern religious practice which laid down that intending communicants, in order to prepare their souls, must starve their bodies and abjure all worldly activities. In my time, all that ever happened in Southend was a holiday and an evening service in the church. Now there is no service, but the holiday remains. We play golf and go for family picnics and otherwise enjoy ourselves. On Sunday we eat the bread and drink the wine. Are our souls less worthy?

On the Fair Days the farm servants used to trudge to Campbeltown, or, if they were lucky, get a lift in a farmer's machine. The town was always busy.

Farmers' ladies sported new hats. Workers and their lasses danced at street corners. Farmers and farm servants got together on 'fee-ing' business. When a farmer contracted to employ a new servant he gave him 'erles', which, fifty years ago, was usually half-a-crown. Like the King's shilling for a new recruit, it was practical evidence that an unbreakable bargain had been struck.

In the evenings competitions for singing and mouth-organ play-ing were held in the Christian Institute. As a rule the winners came from families like the Mitchells and the MacShannons. The MacShannons were descendants of the sennachies who, five hundred years ago, made music for the MacDonalds of the Isles.

The Fair Days offered, of course, magnificent opportunities for getting drunk. This was only natural, considering the drabness of a bygone country life and the fact that whisky and beer cost about a twentieth of what they do now. Long after midnight stumbling legs carried their owners back to the farms. But here the fun ended. The ploughing or the sowing or the work of the harvest had to begin again at first light. There was no escaping the march of the seasons.

Another big day in the lives of my father's parishioners—and in ours as well—was the Ploughing Match. It provided a picture to charm a MacTaggart or a Munnings. The ploughs themselves, single-furrow high-cutters painted red and blue for the occasion, were, as a rule, valued heirlooms in families like the Ronalds and the Galbraiths. Their slender shafts were gripped and guided by white-shirted competitors as teams of Clydesdales, gaily harnessed, thrust mighty shoulders against their drag. Gulls squabbled for worms in the gleaming brown furrows. Distant fields were emerald green against a slate-blue horizon.

The experts had their own particular joy—a day-long argument on the merits and demerits of each competitor, such an argument often sustained by surreptitious nips out of bottles in hedge-shaded corners of the field. But in the end one individual emerged. He was the ploughman whose strong yet delicate hands had fashioned the straightest furrows, turning them over and fitting them to-gether so closely that no trace of green was visible in a design of geometrical precision.

The winner was loaded with prizes, for 'the best lot on the field', 'the best break' and 'the best finish'—and often for 'the competitor with the largest family', because a numerous and hungry family, as in boxing, used to be a considerable factor in the making of a successful ploughman. In any case, we all admired the champion's stamina and dour determination.

Today, of course, the picture of a ploughing match is different. The growl and groan of tractors make conversation difficult. The scent of damp grass and freshly turned earth is obliterated by petrol fumes. A modern competitor requires no stamina, no delicate poise of mind and muscle. He requires, indeed, no outstanding technical skill, because the plough is adjusted and set by his handlers. The quality of his work is a measure of his ability to move certain levers on his tractor.

Older ploughmen—and older spectators, like me—are not enthusiastic about the modern scene. The bitter end for most of us occurred about ten years ago when a girl of fifteen, with a blue ribbon on her pony-tail and a shrewd father at the end of her rig, became a champion.

There's no doubt that the art of ploughing has died the death, like the arts of thatching and of building a dry-stane dyke. In a technological age it was inevitable. I can't help wondering, however, what kind of poems Burns might have composed sitting at the wheel of a rory red tractor. Excellent ones, no doubt, though perhaps written in an up-to-date manner avoiding rhyme and scansion. I'm not sure if they'd have stirred the hearts of us old squares.

My father was minister of Southend for 47 years. In that time he saw a revolution not only in ploughing matches but also in agriculture as a whole. Today most of the local farmers are no longer tenants. The Duke of Argyll sold his Kintyre estates in 1955, and now they own their own farms (along with the shooting and the fishing rights) and run them with great efficiency and profit.

They get about twelve times as much for their milk as they did fifty years ago, and a creamery in Campbeltown does all the butter and cheese making. The men can well afford dinner-jackets and, indeed, often wear them at Burns Suppers, Agricultural Dinners and other rural 'on-gauns'. The ladies, freed from dairy duties by press-button milking-machines and creamery tankers and from uncontrolled child-bearing by an enlightened Health Service and a more sympathetic outlook on the part of husbands, are as emancipated as their town sisters. They wear mini-skirts by day and gowns for nightly revelry. They dash about in cars and play golf on pleasant afternoons. Byre mucking and domestic drudgery provide the stuff of dreams. Or nightmares.

Thanks in some measure to my father's efforts as a county councillor, the farm servants in Southend now live in comfortable houses, and their wages, while still below the national average, give them a chance at least to exist as human beings and not as slaves.

And yet, in those bad old days, when we were small, the men and women we knew, harried and poverty-ridden though they might have been, had the warmth of humanity in them and a kind of vision. Otherwise, I suppose, they couldn't have borne to live at all.

Before World War I, old Neilly lived in a cave on the shore, eking out an existence by working intermittently on the farms and on the roads. He was often in rags. Sometimes, when he had the money, he got drunk, His nature appeared to be sour, inimical, without hope.

But one day in summer, Archie and I sat with him at the mouth of his cave, looking across the North Channel to the round, blue hills of Ireland only seventeen miles away. He was in a better mood than usual as he shaved in cold water with a rusty old razor.

'Some day', he said to us, 'there will be houses for the likes of me, and maybe a helping hand if there's no work to be had. And the way things are going, I'm thinking I'll live to see it.'

Sure enough, he did live to see it, when governments realised at last that ordinary folk are individuals in their own right, each with a spark of divinity in his soul. He lived until he was nearly 90, in a clean and tidy council house belonging to a relative: a bright-eyed, humorous old man, clean-shaven, wearing a neat grey suit and a cloth cap, a much less intimidating character than the one we had known as boys.

But he still remembered the survival techniques of his younger days, and many a valuable hint he gave us on the art of poaching a pheasant or a salmon. (Do you know the best way of poaching a pheasant? It involves the use of paper sweetie-bags and treacle. I'll describe it in more detail, later.)

In spite of all the changes that occurred in Southend during my father's ministry, he used to say that two factors remained constant. Human nature was one, and, as a minister, he spoke from experience about that. The instinct of the born farmer was the other.

The new agricultural science is a valuable aid to intelligent farmers, but unless a man is bred in the country and serves a long apprenticeship he lacks the ingrained knowledge of how to get the best out of his land, of how to judge the weather and the seasons, of how to deal patiently and lovingly with natural things.

Modern methods are good, employed selectively. But old-fashioned ideas don't *all* deserve the dust-bin.

2

The Meaning of Magic

We all loved Southend and still do. As children, our happiest times were when the school closed for holidays in July and December.

Sons of the Manse were supposed to be genteel, and it irked us that when other boys went barefoot in summer we were forced to wear sandshoes. Our village pals, the soles of whose feet were like scarred leather, called us softies, and we had to retaliate in the customary manner, with flying arms and fists. If we were caught fighting, Mr James Inglis Morton, the schoolmaster, gave us the strap, and between one thing and another we had to endure a fair amount of bodily harm. We seldom discussed wounds and bruises with our parents, for the simple reason that my father would have applied the back of a hair-brush to our behinds if he'd known about their origin.

Sometimes, in warm weather, when the fighting and the strapping were over, we sought to immerse our contusions in the healing sea or in the fresh water of the Minister's Lynn. We bathed 'bare scuddy' and only ceased this practice when Rona came along. This had nothing to do with prudery. We put on bathing trunks because my mother bought them for us and explained that Rona might look down her snub, unladylike nose at bathers who resembled woad-covered aborigines.

The Minister's Lynn is a deep pool at a bend of the River Con, which runs through the old glebe land below the Manse. It debouches into a shallow fall, filled with smooth boulders. Here, on a day when the burn was brown with spate, Archie and I learned to swim.

We had built a raft of planks and empty paraffin tins. Lying flat on top of it, like heroes in the *Boys' Own Paper*, we thrust out into the sullenly flowing water of the Lynn. With our hands we paddled strongly towards the opposite bank. Half way across, our ramshackle craft began to break up. We clutched at floating tins, overbalanced and dismally fell overboard.

Puffing, we worked our arms at a vigorous pace. At moments our toes touched the sandy bottom, which gave us, I suppose, a certain amount of confidence. Then there was no bottom, and we were waterborne, striking out calmly and smoothly.

It was strange how it happened to both of us at the same time. We shouted triumphantly to each other and splashed about like porpoises, showing off. We could swim.

The thrill of achievement was to me a kind of pain. Later on I was to speed off on my first bicycle, toe the accelerator of my first fast car and kiss my first girl-friend with intent. The same sharp-edged exhilaration was always present.

But now, blinded with euphoria, Archie and I failed to notice that the current was dragging us towards the fall. One moment the water was beer-brown, sluggish. The next it was a vicious, twisting torrent. White spray pitched against our faces. We gasped for breath. Our bodies jarred and bounced against the rocks. I saw the Manse and the church and the green safety of the glebe whirling high, like a blurred picture in a cinema.

Luckily the fall was gradual and shallow. In a matter of seconds we arrived in a shallow pool thirty yards downstream, bruised, panting, exhausted, but still triumphant.

After that the Minister's Lynn was a place where many youngsters in the parish learnt to swim. Mysterious trees and bushes sprouted from the precipitous bank across the water. Clumps of whins bloomed yellow, their scent bitter-sweet in the hot sun. Birds' nests were common there. The threat to our clothes of bramble thorns and to our health of lurking adders only made the place appear more glamorous and desirable. To reach it on foot, by way of a bridge, involved a walk of nearly a mile. It was imperative that all genuine gang members should be able to make the journey quickly, by swimming.

A few of the boys, including Willie (who was only three), showed

reluctance to brave the deep water. Something had to be done
about this. Like Roman slaves, therefore, the protesters were lined
up and, one by one, hustled down the bank and flung in. Though
the odd individual had to be rescued and hauled ashore, no real
harm came to anybody. Not even to the Cock.

Alec MacCallum was a small, thin boy, the son of a joiner. He
had a bluish complexion, unique in our experience. We understood
vaguely that his heart was weak, but because he was different—
and unable, if provoked, to defend himself—we acted like the
cruel little animals we were and pestered and bullied him. He had
a long neck and a tendency to crow with laughter, so we called
him the Cock. His sister, of course, was the Hen.

Alec had been warned by anxious parents not to overtire himself. Nevertheless, he followed us everywhere, persistently doing
his best to join in the fun.

When the swimming lark began in the Minister's Lynn, he was
one of those who begged leave to be excused: no doubt he had
been told that the shock of bathing in cold water might be
dangerous for him. We deprecated this unorthodox behaviour, but
because Alec was known to be 'delicate', we stopped short of
throwing him into the water like the others.

Being ordinary boys and, therefore, aggressive bullies, we
decided, however, to show our displeasure in a way that was even
more dramatic. We arrested Alec and tried him for cowardice.

The trial took place in our secret headquarters, a disused loft
above one of the Manse outhouses, which we reached by climbing
up through an artificially-enlarged crack in the coal-shed ceiling.
The court assembled in this dingy place, the only light being a
shaft of sunshine spearing through a ventilator. The members
included not only my brother Archie but also Hamish Taylor,
whose nickname was 'Boskers' and who is now Convenor of
Argyll County Council, and Lachie Young, at present Director
of Education in Perthshire. Being the oldest, I was presiding judge.

Evidence was sought from various children, who were syco-
phantic as far as the court was concerned and mindlessly inimical
to poor Alec. It was all interesting and enjoyable, except for the
accused, and the court made no effort to hurry the proceedings.

At last, however, judgment was given. The Cock was found guilty and condemned to be hanged. A rope was thrown over a rafter and a noose prepared.

Alec stared at it, speechless, but I don't think he really believed we were in earnest. I hope not, because, of course, the affair was simply our crude idea of a joke.

As it turned out, the joke was on us.

A voice, hard with authority, came from the coal-shed below. 'What are you boys doing, stuck up there on a lovely afternoon like this?'

When no satisfactory answer was forthcoming my father ordered us to come down.

To his credit, Alec remained silent. But Archie, the honest one, soon blurted out the truth. I felt like a hick sheriff in the presence of an enraged Lord Chancellor.

Boskers, Lachie Young and the others were dismissed, with the promise—never fulfilled—that their parents would be informed of their sinful behaviour. Alec was given a penny and a pat on the head and instructed to walk home, quietly.

Archie and I, having been told how fortunate we were not to be in jail for murder, were led to the piano-stool in the drawing-room. Obedient to a sharp order, we bent across it. Then the door was closed to muffle sounds of distress and a hair-brush was employed with explosive violence.

'What if Alec dies from shock?' said my father, at the end.

We shivered. We felt like dying ourselves.

'From now on you will be kind to him. In this world it is the duty of the strong to protect the weak. Tonight you will pray for him.'

We prayed for him all right, with a fervour inspired not only by the pain in our bottoms but also by the sudden realisation of our guilt.

From then on Alec basked in a glow of popularity. He didn't understand, but he accepted the change with humble happiness. We discovered that he was straightforward and loyal and that we actually liked him.

I'm glad to say that the last time I heard about the Cock he was

hale and hearty, living in Edinburgh, in his spare time a devoted
member of a male-voice choir.

But one thing niggled in my mind. In Archie's, too, I think.
My father was strong and we, in comparison, were weak. Why
did he never think of protecting us? It was a long time before we
understood that the experience of hard discipline can be the best
protection of all from 'the slings and arrows of outrageous
fortune'.

When the American-spawned dirt-track racing became news in the
1920s, it found its way to Southend. The long, curving avenue
from the main gate to the Manse front door looked to us like an
ideal track, though the gravel might be less comfortable to fall on
than fine ash.

We had the enthusiastic support of other boys in the parish.
They brought bits of old bicycles and out of a rusty collection we
made two 'racers'. They had no mudguards. Their front wheels
were '28s', their rear ones '26s'. This gave them a rakish sporting
appearance, which was what we wanted.

At first, falls and crashes on the gravel were frequent and painful, but eventually we became skilful enough to negotiate at speed
even the sharp bend at the bottom right-hand corner of the lawn.
The races became desperate duels in which, if you were losing,
you tried to ram your opponent's rear wheel and throw him off.
No quarter was asked or given. Our parents, though obviously
anxious about our safety, never once attempted to impose a ban
on the performances.

There came a day when we decided that the sport was becoming
stale and that it might be a good idea to give the riders some
passengers to pull.

We discovered the remains of two old prams, repaired and
oiled them and attached them like trailers to the bicycles, the
attachments consisting of pieces of rope taken from the clothes
line in the garden. Then, for a trial run, we put Willie and Rona
into the prams. Willie was about six, Rona an infant two years
old.

I think it was Archie and Lachie Young who rode the bicycles.

I remember acting as starter and noticing, as I dropped the flag, that Maimie was watching from the scullery window. Round the gravel they sped, piston-legs thrusting on the pedals, while Willie and Rona sat petrified behind them. All went well until they reached the bend. At this point, obeying a natural law of dynamics which we had overlooked, the prams swerved and skidded outwards. They teetered, heeled over and finally overturned, catapulting Willie and Rona into the trees and bushes below the avenue.

Maimie—all five feet nothing of her—came charging out of the house. 'Child of the earth,' she screamed at me, 'you've killed them!'

Willie and Rona were howling but unhurt. Maimie gathered them to herself like a hen with chickens, dispensing moral comfort and the peppermint sweets she always kept handy in the pocket of her apron. Then, not so much a hen, more a sergeant-major with delinquent recruits, she marched the rest of us towards the Manse and into the presence of the commanding officer (i.e., my father).

This time the hair-brush was not used. Instead he talked to us with Mosaic authority. As we trembled in our sandshoes, he pointed out that if we wanted to kill ourselves doing dirt-track racing, that was all right by him. Evil became part of the equation when we took the risk of killing somebody else. Men had been granted freedom of the will: they were entitled to go to hell if the prospect pleased them; but they were not entitled to drag others along with them.

I have never forgotten that lecture. I wish certain leaders of our so-called permissive society could have heard it. His exposure of the cold selfishness involved in the doctrine of 'untrammeled personal freedom' was, to say the least, educative.

There was magic for children in a country summer. Even more magical was a country Yuletide.

Long ago children were seldom given presents, except at Christmas. The prospect of receiving gifts, therefore, some wrapped in gaily coloured paper, was the main cause of our excitement.

The religious aspect was explained to us at Sunday School, but in the materialistic world of childhood this seemed unimportant as compared with the joy of acquiring new, gaudy possessions. We felt, too, that the story of the birth of the baby Jesus was probably a kind of fairy tale, not to be taken seriously. Otherwise, how could an underground stable in hot and dusty Bethlehem be represented on greeting cards against a background of snow and holly and robins? Only when my father and mother discovered the confusion in our minds and decided to tell us the more realistic nativity stories which formed part of their Celtic heritage, did we begin to understand the true significance of Christmas.

A joy date in our lives was Boxing day. At half-past three in the afternoon a chocolate coloured Daimler, with steel-studded tyres, arrived at our front door. Out of it, attended by a footman and chauffeur burdened with parcels, would step the Duchess—Ina, Dowager Duchess of Argyll, formerly lady-in-waiting and private secretary to Queen Victoria, now one of my father's parishioners. We would be lined up in the drawing-room to receive her, scrubbed, Eton-collared, hair slicked down with plenty of water.

Almost invariably, to the older members of the family at any rate, she would present a book or jigsaw puzzle, because the proper education of children, in manners and morals if not in political science, was something dear to a Victorian heart. But the books and the puzzles, essentially because of their rarity in our experience, were eagerly accepted. The *Empire Annual for Boys* had a pompous, 'educative' appearance, but its contributors, like Percy F. Westerman and Captain Charles Gilson, told stories of incredible deeds which tended to sublimate our Walter Mitty fantasies. The puzzles might depict Milan Cathedral or the Doge's Palace, but as children of the Manse we were inclined to favour religious subjects, and, in any case, the fitting of the pieces was an amusing exercise in its own right.

The Duchess was a regal lady, who, though old-fashioned in many ways, yet painted her cheeks and used powder, much to our secret astonishment. After the death of her husband, taking a cue from Queen Victoria, she invariably dressed in black. She had been the Duke's third wife, and it was rumoured that the marriage had been arranged by the Queen to solace the declining years of one of her favourite Foreign Secretaries; but all this was irrelevant. She was now the Dowager Duchess of Argyll. Her high position in society made it imperative that her life-style as a dutiful widow should be an example to all.

She was autocratic and seldom failed to get her own way. The parish church, St Blaan's, was built in 1774, at the staggering cost of £333. Its main structure is much admired as an example of late eighteenth century architecture. But a porch built against its western gable about seventy years ago, ordered and paid for by the Duchess against expert advice, has been described by a member of the Royal Commission on Ancient Monuments as 'a Victorian monstrosity'.

But underneath the paint and pomp the Duchess had a kind heart. Each baby that arrived in the Manse was visited and my mother's bed heaped with calf's-foot jelly and other tonic delicacies. Rona's inscribed silver christening bowl, a gift from the Duchess, is now a family heirloom. Its custodian at present is John's second daughter, whose name is also Rona.

I have a book she gave me when it became apparent that, no matter what other job I might do, I was going to write stories.

One Sunday in 1923, when I was fifteen, she summoned me to afternoon tea. She lived about four miles away from the Manse in Macharioch House, above whose ornate front door is carved the inscription, *Parva Domus Magna Quies* ('Small house, great quiet'). As boys learning Latin we used to wonder if the stone-carver had perhaps made a mistake, because the place is enormous, built like a castle, and, indeed, has lately been converted into about half-a-dozen holiday flats. However, we realise now that to a Duke of Argyll, accustomed to live in a Gothic pile like Inveraray Castle, surrounded by wide acres of Highland scenery, Macharioch House might perhaps have appeared insignificant and that, after all, life is a strange, stratified mixture of relative values.

I went on my bicycle. At the time I was a gangling youth striving, for the sake of my parents, to curb socialistic tendencies. But in the event the Duchess charmed my cynical soul with tales of Queen Victoria and her own 'dear Duke' and with a great buzz of intimate gossip about the publishing world in London. (She herself had written and published a two-volume *Memoir* of her late husband). I forgot she was an aristocrat—and therefore a proper subject for obloquy—and we talked together for an hour, like old buddies. She didn't even blink an eye when, using an awkward gesture, I upset a cup of tea on a priceless lace traycloth.

Before I left she gave me the present of a book called *Short Story Writing for Profit* by Michael Joseph, with a foreword by Stacey Aumonier. It was full of practical knowledge, a revelation to an aspiring young writer with airy-fairy ideas.

'Study it closely,' said the Duchess. 'It bears out what her Majesty used to say: "A vivid imagination is all very well, but it must be kept in harness." '

To this day, when it occurs to me that I may be a genius, wasting my time writing for filthy money, I commune with Michael Joseph and Stacey Aumonier and they quickly put me back on the road of discipline and common sense.

Short Story Writing for Profit was published by Hutchinson. That evening, as I cycled away from the 'small house' in a shower of November sleet, I had no premonition that one day the same firm would publish twenty-nine of my own books. (This one is the thirtieth.) What occupied my mind was a sudden realisation that the aristocracy—who, in my adolescent imagination, exploited the workers to ensure a lazy, carefree life for themselves—might not be so bad when you got to know them. As a minister's son and, therefore, classless, might I not become a useful catalyst in the long struggle between the rich and the poor, the privileged and the under-privileged?

This was the idea, banal perhaps to an urban sophisticate but fresh to a fifteen-year-old country boy, which, as I pedalled home from Macharioch, made me forget the cold and the wet and the ignominious spilling of my tea.

There is a Gaelic saying to the effect that the common man is entitled to 'a stick from the wood, a fish from the stream and a deer from the forest'. In my father's hearing it was once described by the Duchess as 'highly objectionable'. It is also objectionable in law. Those who practise what it preaches are called poachers.

My mother, a true blue Tory, agreed with the Duchess, regarding the saying not only as objectionable but also as anarchistic. My father, a true red Celt, had no such qualms. Brought up in the remote terrain of North Uist, untroubled by the near presence of snooping gamekeepers or policemen, he often repeated it to us with a smug smacking of his lips. When the Moderator of the Church of Scotland was staying at the Manse and we poached a salmon for his supper (as told in *Salt in My Porridge*) my father's eye was Nelsonian. Our crime was overlooked and even, by inference, commended.

Sometimes, as autumn darkened towards Christmas, pheasants on the cold hills behind the Manse came into the garden in search of food. They were plump and lively, owned by the visiting shooters who slaughtered them with guns. But in those days I, at least, had no profound respect for the game laws, and a sensible conclusion appeared to be that birds which invaded our garden were fair targets for our pot.

One day in November, long before the salmon-poaching incident, Archie and Willie and I crouched at the bathroom window, one storey up above the garden, and watched the pheasants strutting like royalty under the apple trees. The hens were brown and dowdy, the cocks magnificent with black-ribbed wings and emerald green feathers in their heads and tails. I remembered the wise words of old Neilly in the cave and, supported enthusiastically by my brothers, decided to try out his method of catching them.

Our first visit was to the wee shop in the village. There we produced ha'pennies, extracted with the blade of a knife from our letter-box bank, and asked not for sweeties but for as many paper sweetie-bags as could be spared.

Mrs Galbraith was astonished. She was matronly and kind but had a nervous habit of stuttering when something upset her. On this occasion she stuttered so much that we were sprayed with saliva. Eventually, however, we managed to persuade her that we hadn't signed the pledge as far as sweeties were concerned but

that we wanted the bags to blow up and burst in the ears of
unsuspecting pals at school.

Shaking her head and muttering about 'daft boys', she supplied
our order. We returned to the Manse with a dozen bags stuffed
beneath out jerseys.

Our next care was to filch a can of treacle from the larder
when my mother and Maimie weren't looking. For us, experienced
in the ways of adults, this was easy. Knowing that the *Caledonia*,
pride of the Anchor Line, was due to pass that afternoon between
Sanda and the mainland, headed for America, we waited
until her superstructure began to show east of Dunaverty Rock,
about three miles away. Whereupon, feigning childish excitement,
we shouted for everybody to come and look. As my mother and
Maimie, predictably, rushed out on the lawn to exclaim with
admiration at the grace and beauty of the liner, we crept round
to the other side of the house, secured the can of treacle and went
to the dark corner of an outhouse to prepare our lures.

We twisted and folded the necks of the bags into the shape of
small oil-funnels and then artistically smeared the insides with
treacle. Long minutes drifted past, and by the time we had finished
there was as much treacle on our hands and clothes as on the
bags. In our stomachs, too, because knife-blade loads of treacle
offered tempting interludes of relaxation.

Our final task was to take the baited bags into the garden and
lay them out in what we considered strategic positions underneath
the apple trees. Thereafter we retired to keep watch at the bathroom
window.

We were in the bathroom so long that our parents became curious.
Bouts of diarrhoea had to be invented for Archie and Willie,
while I played the role of a sympathetic big brother helping them
to endure the distressing symptoms.

It was almost dusk, and the tea-hour was approaching, when at
last the pheasants came, leaping and whirring over the wall. For
several minutes they moved about, pecking industriously, apparently determined to ignore the bags. Then our spirits surged. An
adventurous cock began to investigate one of them, beak tenta-
tively probing; and in due course, as Old Neilly had foretold,

his head disappeared into the bag and stuck there. Once, twice, he tried to shake it off. But in the end, while we held our breaths, he slowly squatted on the ground and became still.

We hurried downstairs and into the garden, shaking with excitement. Carefully we stalked our prey. Some of the other birds scattered when they saw us, but the big pheasant stayed motionless.

I pounced. Panting, I twisted his neck and killed him.

Old Neilly had declared that when a pheasant gets the treacle bag stuck on its head, and finds itself in the dark, it imagines night has come and immediately beings to roost. We saw him now as a true prophet.

That was the only game bird we ever caught by this method. My mother was 'sad and ashamed' when told what we had done, as well as 'scandalised' by the condition of our clothes. After she and Maimie had gathered up the remaining bags and made a bonfire of them, she sternly forbade any repetition of such criminal behaviour. My father smiled and said nothing. And, in spite of our fears, we did have roast pheasant for lunch on the following day.

Another method, which has much to commend it, is to scatter corn soaked in whisky so that the pheasants may eat their fill and become intoxicated. When they begin to stagger about they can be pursued and caught without effort. We were never able to put this one to the test, mainly because we couldn't afford to buy whisky.

But the treacle method is effective. We proved it.

There was magic about Christmas at the Manse; but sometimes for us children curious and daunting events occurred in its aftermath.

One example took place when Archie was about two years old and Willie a baby. We were gathered in the dining-room, after breakfast, for Family Worship. My mother was in her usual armchair by the fire, with Willie on her knee. Maimie was perched on a straight-backed chair beside her. I was doing my best to look holy, standing by the window. Archie was on the floor, eyeing the exciting carpentry set he'd got from Santa and wishing it was time to start hammering again.

My father, seated by the table, read a passage from the Bible, continuing, as he did so, to smack his lips in appreciation of the tasty bowl of porridge he had recently consumed. Finally he shut the good book, got up, turned round, knelt by his chair and began, in a loud and unctuous voice, to pray. We all bent our heads—all, it transpired, except Archie. As the prayer went on, he, apparently, became excessively bored. Unseen by any of us, he lifted his toy hammer and toddled across to a position immediately behind my father. Then, taking careful aim at the bald spot, he struck.

'Buck up!' he piped, using a catch-phrase of the time often used by Maimie and our parents.

That morning there may have been laughter in heaven: there was none in the Manse. My father's reaction to sudden, unexpected pain was so awful, so blasphemous even, that it is better left unrecorded. Enough to say that the meaning of his pulpit phrase, 'the wrath of God', at last became clear to me.

I can't remember exactly when Family Worship in the Manse ceased to be held. Possibly the crack of Archie's hammer signalled a decline in my father's enthusiasm for an ancestral ritual. By the time Rona and the others came along all week-day praying was done in private. I don't think our Christian beliefs were diminished on this account.

More than a decade later we lived through another post-Christmas 'happening'. In this case the juvenile leads were Willie, Rona and Kenneth. (John was still hovering off-stage.)

My father had been a chaplain during World War I and by now was known to his family—and to everyone else in the parish—as the Padre. A veteran of the Salonika campaign, he had begun to indulge in a snooze after lunch, a Churchillian habit which no doubt contributed to his longevity. That afternoon, as usual, he went upstairs to the bedroom and settled himself comfortably under the quilt. For some reason he failed to shut the door.

It was the week after Christmas, and Willie, Rona and Kenneth were playing in the hall below with a toy cart that had been Kenneth's present from the Duchess. An exciting idea occurred to them.

In those pre-Rob days we had a cat, whose name was Ginger. What a marvellous thing it would be, they thought, if Ginger could be yoked to the cart and persuaded to do her stuff as a horse.

Willie soon located her, drowsing by the kitchen fire. My mother and Maimie, washing dishes in the scullery, failed to notice what was going on.

Struggling and scratching, Ginger was held firmly by Willie, while Rona and Kenneth, with bits of string, attached her to the cart. Finally they let her go.

Instead of moving sedately around the hall, as had been expected, an enraged and insulted cat rushed upstairs, yowling, dragging the cart behind her. Willie and the others, in dismay, galloped after her, a desperate thought pricking their imaginations.

The thought came true. Into the parental bedroom fled Ginger, the clatter of the trailing cart disturbing dreams. Jerking upright, the Padre saw a nightmare beast flash across the floor in front of him and then, in a flurry of soot, disappear up the chimney.

That is to say, Ginger disappeared. Her appendage remained in view, and the truth dawned on all concerned that the cat and cart were now dangling on opposite sides of the steel backing in the fireplace. Judging by Ginger's muffled yells, she was in danger of being strangled by the string yoke.

The Padre remained in bed, but his shouts brought the entire household to his aid. Maimie scuttled about the bedroom, swearing in the Gaelic, replying in kind to the barbed words of the Padre. Archie and I stood just within the threshold, keeping open a line of retreat. Willie, Rona and Kenneth, tugging at the cart, tried to give the impression of being helpful. My mother, surveying with pity the man in the bed, was the only one who did anything. She found a pair of scissors on the dressing-table, pushed aside her younger offspring, stretched up into the chimney and cut the string.

The cart fell into the grate. The cat stopped yelling. For a moment there was silence.

Then Ginger again took charge. Leaping up from behind the fireplace backing, she scrambled and slithered down into the grate, saw a crowd of people blocking the direct line to the door and decided on another route straight over the bed. She jumped and bounced across the Padre, showering him with soot, swerved past Archie and me at the door and went downstairs like a shooting star with a black tail.

Archie and I followed her. So, with prudent haste, did Rona, Kenneth and Maimie.

'My clean sheets!' I heard my mother cry.

'Sheets!' came a voice from the bed. 'What about me?'

Then, we are told, the Padre noticed Willie, who was gazing at him, fascinated. 'You're to blame for this!' he roared. 'Come here!'

At first, like a snake confronted by a mongoose, Willie didn't move. But when the quilt was thrown aside and the man beneath erupted on to the floor, he finally took steps to protect himself. Dodging round the Padre, he escaped from the room, flew along the corridor outside and locked himself in the bathroom.

In long drawers and grey hand-knitted socks, a Black and White Minstrel hammered at the door. 'Open up!' he ordered.

But Willie pretended not to hear. In the bathroom he stayed until the tornado blew itself out, as, from experience, he knew it would within a calculable time.

On my mother's instructions, the incident was never mentioned again in the presence of the Padre. He was a human being, she pointed out, as well as a minister.

This truth was difficult for children to understand. When we did come to understand it, when we finally realised what personal sacrifices he and my mother must have made in order to give us all a good upbringing, both moral and material, on an annual stipend beginning at £180 and never exceeding £600, our filial regard burgeoned into a love and respect which made temporary uproars and administrations of discipline seem trivial punctuation marks in the family history. Maimie's example of unselfish service, despite her frequent habit of assaulting us with both words and fists, also helped to provide a sense of values which I think we have found of benefit.

As a rule, today's children receive a better education than we did. Their sports and games are more thoroughly organised. Their standards of fitness, thanks in part to scientifically planned school meals, are higher than ours were. For these advantages they are indebted, in the main, to the Welfare State, that magnificent conception of mutual aid which has transformed the lives of millions. But the Welfare State, in its present form of administration, has one defect which has put modern children at a psychological disadvantage unknown to us.

They are brought up without the necessity of doing much or even thinking much for themselves. Almost inevitably they tend to believe that they have a divine right to it all, that they can afford to sit back and enjoy themselves while everything is done for them by others.

Some modern parents appear to take delight in encouraging this belief. Carefully they protect their offspring from the cruel knowledge that nobody has a divine right to anything, and that, contrary to a mushy modern philosophy, the world does *not* owe them a living and that, sooner or later, if they want privileges, they must earn them.

The Welfare State exists only because there are enough hard-working people in the country willing to pay for it. The government has no private treasure-chest: it gets the money out of which benefits are paid from those who are taxpayers and rate-payers. At some point in their lives modern children come face to face with the awkward proposition that in life there must be 'give' as well as 'take', that instead of the world owing them a living they themselves owe the world a great deal for being alive at all.

It depends largely on their upbringing how they react. Nowadays it seems to me that too many react in outbursts of bitter and sometimes violent behaviour. Characters pampered in childhood shiver and scream at the first blast of a cold wind. The happy people—the lucky people—are those reared to endure discipline and to understand the point of view of their elders. When the crunch comes, it is nothing new in their experience and they can cope with it, sensibly.

For some young people disillusionment occurs when they go to the University. There they discover that nobody worries about their attendance record or cares in the least about their moral or physical welfare, except in an abstract kind of way. So they dance all night and sleep all day. They drink coffee and eat chocolate biscuits. They talk interminably about pop art and pop politics, canoodle in the back seats of the stalls and experiment with pints and 'pot'. But at the end of the first year they fail their exams. Grants and bursaries are taken from them. They are miserable and lonely and hate themselves.

I know. In spite of my advantages I went through it.

Generally, the first year away from home and school is the testing time. Youngsters who fail the test become disgruntled moaners clutching at every chance to make a quick buck out of social security —that is, at the expense of their neighbours.

Those who succeed translate the disciplines taught by parents and teachers into self-discipline. They come to terms with the fact that the world is not really divided into three separate classes —teen-agers, middle-agers and old age pensioners—but that these descriptive labels have been invented for commercial and political purposes and that we are all just people, dependent on one another for survival, with everybody, including teen-agers and old age pensioners, required to 'give' as well as 'take'. They begin to understand that what leads to the good life is not being 'with it' in a material sense but that the old-established virtues of kindness, tolerance and temperance (in its widest sense) are the corner stones of happiness.

They reach the inescapable conclusion, too, that parents and teachers are only human and therefore liable to make mistakes, but that in spite of what may appear to be stupid and repressive conduct they are always firmly on the side of youth.

Fortunately, in spite of what we read in the newspapers, the young people who pass the test far outnumber those who don't.

Had we been forced, as children, to listen to a lecture on the lines of the above, we should proabably have described it as a load of cod's-wallop. But though we weren't aware of it at the time, our parents—and Maimie —continued to teach us never to wait for Godot, never to wait for somebody else to do something for us. They did it because they loved us and had a care for our future well-being.

We are grateful to them.

3

Down to Earth

The Padre and my mother (Maimie, too) were born in crofting and farming communities. They were country folk, unsophisticated, uncomplicated. I suppose that, being their children, any sophistication we may claim is a thin veneer.

The Celtic culture, in which they were nourished, was simpler and earthier than that found in southern regions. For example, the Anglo-Saxon influences which governed the celebration of Christmas, even in a remote country parish like Southend, were, at first, strange to them.

Most of the hymns and carols sung by the choir had an alien ring. *The First Nowell, It Came upon the Midnight Clear* and *In the Bleak Midwinter* were Old English. *While Humble Shepherds Watched Their Flocks, Still the Night* and *From Heaven Above to Earth I Come* were German. The only purely Hebridean hymn my father could find in the Church Hymnary was *Child in the Manger*, a poem written over a hundred years ago by Mary MacDonald, a crofter's wife who lived in Bunessan in Mull. The melody, he discovered, was also Hebridean, so old that its origins were forgotten.

Old the melody may be, but it still lives on, not only as a hymn but also as a chart-topping number called *Morning is Broken*.

Personally, I have nothing against the Anglo-Saxon hymns and carols; but I agree with the opinion of my parents that they emanate a certain sophistication, a certain preoccupation with material things like snow and harps of gold and frankincense and myrrh that somehow takes away from the simiplicity of the painful birth of a baby in a stable. Ordinary human feelings, ordinary human anxieties are veiled in a flurry of tinsel.

But in the seasonal stories told us by our parents in those pre-television days, this romantic image was less apparent. In my view —though I am, of course, prejudiced—they reveal much more of the root meaning of Christmas.

An old poem from Benbecula, translated from the Gaelic by Alexander Carmichael, compiler of *Carmina Gadelica*, may illustrate what I mean.

> Joseph and Mary went
>   To the numbering up,
> And the birds began chorusing
>   In the wood of the turtle doves.
>
> The two were walking the way
>   Till they reached a thick wood,
> And in the wood there was fruit
>   As red as the rasp.
>
> That was the time when she was great,
>   When she was carrying the King of grace,
> And she took a desire for the fruit
>   That was growing on the gracious slope.
>
> Then spoke Mary to Joseph,
>   In a voice low and sweet,
> 'Give to me of the fruit, Joseph,
>   That I may quench my desire.'
>
> And Joseph spoke to Mary,
>   And the hard pain in his breast,
> 'I will give thee of the fruit, Mary,
>   But who is the father of thy burden?'
>
> Then it was that the babe spoke,
>   From out of her womb,
> 'Bend ye down every beautiful bough
>   That my Mother may quench her desire.'
>
> And from the bough that was highest
>   To the bough that was lowest
> They all bent down to her knee,
>   And Mary partook of the fruit
>   In her loved land of prophecy.

> Then Joseph said to Mary
> And he full of heavy contrition
> 'It is carrying *Him* thou art,
> The King of Glory and of grace?
> Blessed art thou, Mary,
> Among the women of all lands!'

Here is beauty, but earthiness, too: a recognition that though Joseph was in love with his wife he must also have been jealous and afraid. Joseph has been neglected in the literature of Christmas, and his natural human reaction to the possibility that his wife was going to have an illegitimate child has often been glossed over or camouflaged. Not, however, in the Hebrides.

There is a legend of Celtic hospitality, especially around Christmas time. Hospitality, of course, is not peculiar to the Celts, though sometimes we try to persuade ourselves that it is. Spontaneous kindness is just as common in London and Rome, India and Madagascar. After all, Jock Tamson's bairns are international. But I do think the Celts have a warmth of hospitality which is difficult to find elsewhere, and this may be due to St Columba, whose example has still a powerful influence in Ireland and Scotland.

In the week before Christmas, more than fourteen hundred years ago, Columba and his monks on Iona had no shopping to do, no feverish business deals to worry them, no forgotten presents to buy, no last-minute cards to send. They could concentrate on receiving visitors, and no matter who those visitors might be, holy men or lepers, rich men or poor, they were all immediately happed around with kindness.

First they were taken to the church, there to give thanks for a safe journey. Then they were escorted to the guest-house, where either Columba himself or one of his monks knelt down and washed their feet. Finally, even though it happened to be a Fast Day, they were given a meal, before which a blessing was said. A blessing like this:

> Each meal beneath our roof,
> They will all be mixed together,
> In the name of God the Son,
> Who gave them growth.

Milk and eggs and butter,
The good produce of our own flock,
There should be no dearth in our island,
Nor in our dwelling.

I will sprinkle water on them all,
In precious name of the Son of God,
In name of Mary the generous
And of Patrick.

The inspiration of Celtic generosity to a stranger is probably the story of 'no room at the inn'. A pregnant woman, obviously near her time, came to a house in Bethlehem and was refused admittance. It was unthinkable that such a thing should ever happen again. So, no matter what kind of person knocks at the door, a wearer of rags or somebody scarred with disease, he must never be turned away, because here may be Christ again, in the guise of a stranger.

The European legends of Christmas have little to say about Joseph. Not much more about Mary and her feelings as a young woman about to give birth to her first child. Nor do they deal much with the practical, troublesome and painful business of having a baby, without medical help, in a dark, unhygienic stable. The storytellers are too concerned with the symbolic side of it: the star in the east and the three wise men with their lavish gifts.

The Celtic legends are much more down to earth, more human, I think. One of them is about St Bride, the midwife or 'aid woman', as for centuries she has been called in the Gaelic.

Bride, Bride! Come in,
The welcome is truly made.
Give thou relief to this woman
And give the conception to the Trinity.

The story goes that Bride (or Bridget) came from a poor family and was a servant at the inn in Bethlehem. It was she who answered the door when the two strangers asked for shelter. It was she who had to tell them there was no room inside.

But she saw that they were tired and hungry and that the

lovely young woman, with the 'gold brown hair hanging to her waist', was near the end of her pregnancy. So, being warm-hearted, she showed them to the stable and said they could rest there. She brought the woman her own frugal supper, 'a stoup of water and a bannock of bread'.

And soon afterwards, when Mary's time came, Bride was with her, to help and give comfort and receive the child into her arms.

Then, according to the story, Bride put three drops of water on the baby's forehead, in the name of God, in the name of Christ, in the name of the Spirit.

Here is the traditional prayer of a Hebridean woman in labour:

> Come to my help,
>   Mary fair and Bride.
> As Anna bore Mary,
>   As Mary bore Christ,
> As Eile bore John the Baptist
>   Without flaw in him,
> Aid thou in my unbearing,
>   Aid me, O Bride!

The story of Christmas adapted to Anglo-Saxon tastes is foreign to Celtic realism.

When good King Wenceslaus looked out on Bohemian snow and feasted comfortably on Bohemian food and wine—and, since he could afford such luxuries, who can blame him?—ragged Hebridean children went from door to door among the smoke-filled 'black houses', singing Christmas songs for crusts of bread. If there was a baby in the house they would take it for a symbolic Christ-child and carry it three times round the fire which burned in the middle of the floor, singing in Gaelic their home-made carols. If there was no baby they would improvise a lay figure and do the same. In return, the man of the house would give them scraps of bread to eat, sometimes with pieces of crowdie cheese.

A baby, unadorned by the trappings of romance, unconcealed by the rich vestments of liturgy. This was the traditional concern of the Celts. This was also the background out of which came my father's call to the ministry.

The Rev. Angus John MacVicar, MA, JP, to give him his full title, was a minister in the Church of Scotland for 63 years. He was born in North Uist, on 23 June 1878, in a 'black house' thatched with heather and straw, where a peat fire smouldered on the kitchen floor and the smoke escaped through a hole in the roof.

His father and mother were crofting folk, Gaelic speakers whose only education had been Bible training in church schools. He was five years old before he could speak English. To the end his speech contained traces of the Gaelic idiom, as in his references to 'brain-scattered' instead of 'scatter-brained' and in advice to his children never to put 'the horse before the cart'. My mother told him once I was making a great 'song and dance' about being forced to attend a boring function in the church hall. He fixed me with a glittering eye: 'Do what you're told, Angus, and stop making a dance and song!'

Perhaps it was a legacy of poverty which made him determined to acquire a University degree and become a minister and which aroused his social conscience to such an extent that all his life he fought hard in county councils and education committees for better housing, better medical facilities and better education for his parishioners.

No ivory tower for him. No intellectual sermon on a Sunday and a vague hand of blessing on a child's head during a time-table 'visitation'. He was in there fighting all the time, in church or market, on Sundays and week-days, full of charm one moment and of irascibility the next, arguing the toss for practical Christianity.

Basically he had the Christian virtue of humility; but he was never one to camouflage truth with mock modesty. The author of *The Road to the Isles*, the Rev. Kenneth MacLeod, became minister of Gigha and a member of Kintyre Presbytery some time after my father was appointed Clerk in 1912. With a glint of mischief in his deep dark eyes he used to recall for my benefit a question he'd asked the Padre: 'Angus, why do you think they made you Clerk?' To which a reply had come simply: 'Where could they have found a more suitable man?'

My brother Kenneth, on being ordained, naturally asked his

father for some advice on the subject of the parish ministry. The answer he got had a double edge. 'Always be at your best at a funeral,' the Padre told him, 'because that is the time you'll get nearest to your people and be able to offer the most comfort. Another thing. You're bound to make enemies in your parish, Kenneth, if you have a spark of character at all. But don't worry about it. The chances are you'll bury most of them!'

In his young days he was a keen shinty player, the first captain of the Glasgow University Shinty Club when it was founded in a pub at the corner of Gibson Street in 1901. A great team man and, according to his contemporaries, a dangerous opponent, liable to wield his *caman* with more enthusiasm than gentle care. This, of course, was characteristic. He saw a goal and made straight for it, scorning devious politics and any compromise with the opposition. If he got hurt in the process, as he often did, that was simply part of the game called life.

Susan, Willie's youngest daughter, currently a medical student at Glasgow University, plays hockey for Scotland. Marsali, John's eldest daughter, has done so, too, as a schoolgirl. Did they inherit their skilful stick-swinging from the Padre?

One humiliating blow, as he approached the age of 60, was his failure to learn how to drive a car. I was abroad at the time, just after the war, but I got the story from John, then a nineteen-year-old medical student who had been appointed instructor. (A more unenviable task would be hard to imagine.)

His pupil, as he soon discovered, had no mechanical bent. The internal combustion engine and the theory and practice of power transmission were of even less interest to him than what he called 'those blasted ecumenical committees'. His mind was on higher things, such as trying to subdue a recalcitrant steering-wheel.

For days John sat in the passenger-seat, enduring liver-shaking buffets as the Padre strove to master the clutch and suffering terror as his pupil, snarling blasphemies at the pedals below, took his eye off the road and headed for walls and hedges. Anything the Padre did wrong he blamed on John, whose patience, according to himself, was a superb mixture of Stoicism and Christianity. (I can imagine John's wife and young family being sceptical about this!)

Weeks passed, and there was no improvement. It appeared that even Celtic imagination and endurance were no match for the mechanical cussedness of an Austin 7.

The end came on a bright autumn evening when John took him out with a view to his driving 'round the hill', on a road with many twists and one particularly sharp right-angled turn. Unfortunately this turn was preceded by a steep upward slope which necessitated a change of gear. Here occurred Armageddon. With bangs and crashes—and loud invocations to the Almighty—the Padre succeeded in changing gear, but the effort caused him to forget about the wheel. Instead of gracefully rounding the bend the car screamed across the road, bucked at a violent application of the brakes, and then nose-dived into a ditch.

Pupil and instructor slowly regained breath. Then—'John, you fool,' roared the Padre, 'why didn't you tell me to turn the wheel?'

Thereafter, as before, he went about his parochial duties on his old bicycle.

And yet, despite his foibles—and encouraged, I know, by my mother's miraculous faith and understanding—he inspired many besides his own family to follow and fight with him. He was never a man apart, as some ministers tend to become when they find the world and its worldliness too difficult to cope with. The hard realism of his Hebridean ancestors prevented this. He marched with his people and shared their trials, for 47 years as their minister and for another 14 as a retired friend living in their midst.

It is said that St Columba and his disciples, before they went to Iona in 563, first landed in Scotland on the shore at Southend. What are called St Columba's Footsteps are still to be seen on a knoll near the graveyard of Keil-colm-cille. Though archaeologists date one at least of the Footsteps from the first millennium BC, and describe the rock on which they are carved as a place where pagan chiefs once swore fealty to their tribe, it is probable that Columba also used them as a pulpit, while preaching his new Christianity on a text of old Druidism.

His message contained echoes of paganism. A statesman as well as a churchman, he built the new faith on the foundation of the

old, just as missionaries in Africa often erect their churches in
the so-called holy places of the witch-doctors. He acknowledged
that the former religion of fear—fear of darkness and of death, of
winters which might never change to summer—had some logic in
it. Nature was cruel and had to be appeased: it was a physical
fact of life.

Then, having acknowledged this, he would send his big voice
sounding against the cliffs at Keil: 'But fear can be overcome, as
day overcomes night, as summer overcomes winter. I bring you a
gospel not only of the body but of the spirit. Your Druids utter
words of faith and hope. But now I give you another word, the
word of *my* Druid, whose name is Christ. A word that is strong
and full of magic and can cast out fear. That word is love.'

The Padre was a true follower of St Columba, preaching the
gospel of Christ in everyday living. He pedalled for miles on his
ancient bicycle, visiting the old and the sick, the young and the
troubled. He seldom took a holiday. When he left his parish it was
either to preach for a clerical friend or to attend a county council
meeting.

For a man reared in what we, as children, imagined must have
been a strict and inhibiting Presbyterian atmosphere, he had a
remarkably tolerant attitude to sins of the flesh. (My mother had
the same, but they saddened her more than they did the Padre.)
Couples living in sin, illegitimate children, intermittent drunkeness
—examples of all these were as common in Southend as elsewhere;
but he made no great 'dance and song' when they were brought to
his notice. He gave the individuals words of warning but was at
pains, in private and in the pulpit, to remind them that the Church's
arms are always open and forgiving.

His approach to people who sinned with calculation was inimical. Towards those who went 'a kennin' wrang', in the Burnsian
sense, he acted with humanity, possibly aware of his own fleshly
lusts and recognising that but for the grace of God he might have
been a greater delinquent himself.

Was this tolerance a legacy from earthy Celtic ancestors who
could look the facts of nature in the face and still believe in the
triumph of good over evil? Whatever its origin, we all benefited

from its example and, I believe, inherited our share of it. We found no puritanical difficulties in contemplating violence, sex or drink.

Our parents allowed us to practice the natural violence of childhood and, through painful experience, we learned that in order to achieve a good life violence must be contained by spiritual discipline. I believe it was a proper training. Violence in man is as natural as storm and tempest. How can children—or adults —come to terms with it unless they have some experience of its consequences?

In the countryside of Southend the business of sex went on around us, practised openly by the fowls in the farmyard and the cattle and sheep in the fields. We discussed it with our pals at school and older acquaintances after school. We learnt to appreciate old Charlie's joke about 'the older the fiddle the sweeter the tune' and, for some obscure reason, equated it in our youthful minds with Browning's 'Grow old along with me, the best is yet to be'.

Nobody, least of all our parents, tried to shelter us from sex. When we became adolescents we saw the green shoots thrusting up from the damp earth. We smelt the acridity of spring. We became aware of a girl's delicate skin and the curve of her breasts and hips and, within ourselves, experienced the stirrings of lustful energy. But it didn't take us by surprise. Nor did it make us feel guilty, because we knew it was a powerful coil in the spring of life.

On the other hand, we saw mothers calling at the Manse with weeping daughters, bulkily clad, and were thereby warned of the sad consequences of undisciplined indulgence.

As far as drink was concerned, we were allowed to know that my father took a dram, though sparingly. When old enough to visit the bar at the inn we did so. If we drank too much we vomited and our potency with the girls was diminished, all of which, in the natural course of events, restricted our intake. Lack of money was another factor in the formation of reasonably temperate habits.

My future brother-in-law, Archie McKerral, occupied a farm 'round the hill'. He was a bachelor, a wonderful singer of Scots songs and a constant visitor at the Manse. One day in the summer holidays, when I was approaching 19, I helped him to drive half-a-dozen of his stirks to market in Campbeltown. Today they would travel in a motor-float, but in those difficult times for agriculture they—and we—walked every yard of the ten miles. As it turned out, Archie's beasts fetched good prices. Tired, hot and triumphant, we adjourned to a nearby pub to celebrate.

This was about half-past five in the afternoon. At nine o'clock we were still there. Singing 'like a lintie', Archie was entertaining the customers. Free drinks were raining down on us.

I went to the urinal to empty my churning stomach and distended bladder. I was standing there, preparing to fasten my flies, when a small pale man with spectacles came in. He grinned at me, sidled across and began to finger my private parts. It might not have been such a shock had he been a stranger. In fact I knew him quite well as a member of a respectable Campbeltown family.

This was one aspect of life for which I was unprepared. Acting instinctively, like a frightened colt, I lashed out and struck him in the face. He fell, sprawling on the urine-wet tiles, his spectacles broken beneath him.

I got Archie out of the bar and we set out on the long, sobering journey home. I was shaking, as if I'd seen a ghost.

Next day I pumped up courage and told the Padre what had happened. He didn't blink an eye. He made no mention of the devil drink. He didn't even refer to Sodom and Gomorrah. Instead, he said something like this: 'You and I are lucky, Angus. We can take a dram and leave it and our sexual desires are normal. It's the way we're made, and we should be thankful for it. But there are plenty of people in the world whose reaction to drink is a craving for more and more. These are the alcoholics. They are victims of a disease and are no more to blame for their condition than haemophiliacs. There are also plenty of people whose sexual desires are abnormal. A woman has no appeal to them. Their desire is for another man. These are the homosexuals. We've got to learn to live with them and help them if we can, because they are human beings. Last night you acted in an uncivilised way. First of all you got drunk, deliberately. Then you struck a fellow man in anger. It won't do, Angus.'

'But that man interfered with me. I reacted on instinct. What else could I have done to stop him?'

He smiled, suddenly. 'What a friend of mine in the Lovat Scouts once did in the same circumstances. Told him to bugger off!'

No doubt members of our family have all sinned in the areas of violence, sex and drink. I know I have. But I believe the sins would have been greater and more traumatic had it not been for the tolerance of our parents.

The Padre's attitude to superstition was the same as Columba's. From his Celtic ancestors he had inherited a good deal of it himself, and his way was not to condemn it but to try and absorb it in the Christian pattern.

Not long after he came to Southend he was called to the deathbed of an old man who'd been a tinker. The house was damp and dark and cold. A candle stood in its wax on a packing-case by the bed. Its flame stirred in the draught from a window stuffed with rags. The old man's daughter, a widow of nearly 70, was the only other person there.

My father shivered in his overcoat. The night went on into morning, but the old man in the straw bed stayed silent, his breathing slow and shallow.

Then the daughter, whose name was Phemie, touched my father's arm. 'It's his time!' she whispered.

The old man was moving painfully, trying to speak. All my father could hear were the words: 'The earth, Phemie. The earth.'

Now, for the first time, he noticed on the mantelpiece a saucer containing a white-brown mixture. His mind went back to North Uist to a story about his own maternal grandfather, who, though an elder of the Church, had asked at the end for 'the earth and the salt', symbols of a pagan ritual as old as time.

The daughter looked at the saucer, then at my father. He nodded. She took it and laid it on her father's breast. And as the Padre prayed, the withered flesh ceased to move and the shallow breathing stopped.

He drew no lessons from this. The earth and the salt, the bread and the wine: was there all that much difference?

Sandy Ronald, who leased a sunny farm on the south coast of the parish, opposite the island of Sanda, was accustomed in the early spring to visit what is known in Southend as the Rat Stane. A stumpy pillar of sandstone about three feet tall, with a flat top hollowed into the shape of a font, it stands among the bent a few yards above the shoreline. A local saying has it that 'frae the Rat Stane tae the Gull's Face (a prominent cliff on Sanda) is a couple o' mile exactly.'

(In my unscholarly ignorance, I was slow to realise that the word 'Rat' has nothing to do with the rodents which inhabit nearby caves. During World War II, in Germany, I came across the term 'Raathaus", meaning Council Chamber or Town Hall, and it immediately occurred to me that old Sandy's Rat Stane must have been a meeting place for tribal councils, probably during the Norse occupation of the West of Scotland a thousand years ago.)

Like generations of his predecessors on the farm, old Sandy believed the stone to be an altar of fertility. Every year, in February, he made a pilgrimage to the shore and placed a bright new pin in the 'font'. It was his way of offering a sacrifice to the earth-mother, so that his fields and cattle might be fertile in the coming year. The rough-hewn interior of the 'font' was stained with the rust of many pins.

More than once he brought my father with him on his pilgrimage, confident that one Church of Scotland minister at least would utter no diatribe against idolatry. At the same time, the Padre used to ask him, dryly, if he might not be chancing his luck by having a foot in two camps, pagan and Christian.

My father continued to build his faith—still new in the history of mankind, even after 2000 years—on the foundation of the old.

No parent seeking baptism for a child was ever turned away by him, because, as he said in one memorable sermon: 'The glory of the Church of Scotland is that it always responds to a cry for help, no matter from whom it may come—rich man, poor man, beggarman or thief, sour agnostic or ranting hypocrite.' Angus became the name of several tinker babies, and the drawing-room carpet in the Manse was often wet after he had sloshed water (at times much needed) on their unsuspecting heads.

There was an old farmer in Southend from whose women-folk my mother often bought butter and cheese. He was rough, quick to anger, with a hard honesty which seldom took account of the feelings of others. A terror on the golf course, he strode round the links with half-a-dozen hickory shafted clubs tied together with string.

He often came to the Manse to debate politics with the Padre, emphasising points by beating his stick on the dining-room table. At such moments his grey beard would bristle and his eyes stare like those of a bloodthirsty savage. Cringing behind the door, Archie and Willie and I sometimes feared for our parent's safety; but we learnt, in time, that far from being annoyed the old farmer was thoroughly enjoying the argument. So, I believe, was the Padre.

When well over eighty he became ill and lay lonely and quiet in a 'set-in' bed.

One day the Padre was sent for. He found the daughter puzzled and anxious.

'I don't know what's worrying my father. He won't tell us. He says he'll tell nobody but you.'

The Padre was shown into the bedroom and left alone with him.

'Minister, am I going to die?' No bluster, no anger. Sunken eyes no longer aggressive.

'I don't think you're going to die.' The minister played his part. 'You're too sinful and tough for that!'

'Ay, I'm a sinner.' There was a long pause. Then a frail finger beckoned the Padre closer. 'Will you christen me?' he whispered.

'Christen you? Weren't you baptised, as a child?'

'No. They forgot.' He stirred again, became restless. 'It has bothered me all my life. Now I'm afraid to die without being christened.'

'I can put that right.'

'Can you, minister? But you'll keep it a secret from the family?'

'All right.'

'I don't want them to know. I don't want them to be ashamed.'

There was a cup of water on a table by the bed. My father used it to climax a short christening service in which he and the old farmer were the only participants. It was stretching the rules, but the Padre didn't worry about that, because it gave the dying man happiness.

He lived a little longer, and the water sprinkled on his white head seemed to work a change. Loud invective became meekness, irritable argument peace.

The Manse door was open to girls and young men who had gone wrong, as the ethics of the time would have it. My father married them privately at the Manse—while we stood happily in the wings, armed with rice for throwing at the couple when they left—and made it clear to them that in his opinion a 'sin of love' was on the whole less heinous than a 'sin of hypocrisy'.

Drunk men came to unburden their souls to him, and afterwards my mother and Maimie would supply further therapy in the form of tea and aspirins. Old age pensioners sent for him to sign papers, though what they really wanted was the chance of a 'crack' and some cheerful encouragement from the minister. The unemployed consulted him about jobs. The Duchess consulted him about improvements to the church. With them all he was remarkably patient, though it must be admitted that when the 'unco guid' came to call, spreading calumny about their neighbours, they sometimes got short shrift.

When he became very old and had given up riding a bicycle, he still stumped about the parish on his feet, exchanging gossip with everybody, no doubt a considerable thorn in the flesh of his colleague and successor. But the Rev. James Marks was tolerant and forebearing. Even under the assaults of the Padre's frequent 'good advice' he continued to show a Christian spirit. (I'm afraid that if the circumstances had been reversed my father might not have been so long-suffering.)

My mother's death in 1963 was a sore blow to him. She had been his right hand, guiding his passionate Celtic nature into disciplined channels and attending to his physical needs with endless care. Now the business of looking after him fell upon the family, for Maimie had died, too, some years before my mother. Because we lived near him in Southend Jean and I shouldered most of it. We were assisted by Mrs Julia Yool, who proved not only a neat and tidy housekeeper but also an understanding human being. In the circumstances her gift of humour was what Maimie used to call 'a God's blessing'.

I don't think the Padre was afraid to die, though he loved life so much that even after my mother's death he was never overtly enthusiastic about giving it up. But he faced the prospect with all the earthy courage of his forebears.

He and I often discussed the details of his funeral. The talk would sometimes end with a joke about a great uncle of his in North Uist. On his deathbed the old man spoke to his son. 'And remember the way of Columba, Donald. A dram for the mourners at the house, another on the road to Carinish (the churchyard) and yet another at the graveside.' By this time enthusiasm had put a happy gleam into the old man's eyes. 'And don't forget, Donald, another dram on the way home. And if I'm spared and well myself I'll see to it they get a bumper back here at the house!'

The Padre gave love and got it back in spiritual and physical terms; and at the end of the day the score was settled.

On 30 September, 1970, his body lay in the chancel, below the pulpit from which he had so often preached for 60 years. The church was full. The congregation included not only his old parishioners and friends (many of them Roman Catholics) but also Mohammedans and atheists and a number of folk from the parish who had never been in church before. He would have been glad to see it. Indeed, I felt his eye on me all the time and made certain, on that account, that the funeral arrangements were all he could have wished. ('Dignity and order, Angus. That's the watchword.')

He never opted out of the hurly-burly of living. His religion was practical, straight-eyed like that of his ancestral Celts. But always, behind the practicality, there existed in his eyes the awareness of a vision.

Tir nan Og, perhaps. The land over the horizon. The Celtic land of the Ever Young.

4

Old Masters at the Manse

The Padre loved his elders. Most of them had long beards and, as boys, we thought of them as being fantastically old. I am astonished to realise that fifty years ago most of them were younger than I am now.

Every year, the week before Christmas, he and my mother used to invite them to the Manse for supper. Ostensibly, the purpose of the meeting was to examine the session minutes and approve the church accounts. Such business, however, would be dealt with in a few minutes and the rest of the evening spent in discussing parish history. Archie and Willie and I would be allowed in, 'if we behaved ourselves'. We would sit in a dark corner, well away from the yellow glow of the paraffin lamp on the table, listening with alert ears to stories about old Southend.

At half-time my mother's soda scones, braised ham and gooseberry jelly would disappear from the dining-room table 'like snow off a dyke'. ('A cup of tea in the hand' would have been an insult to country appetites.)

The elders I remember best were the five Archies—Archie MacKay, Archie McCaig, Archie McInnes, Archie McCorkindale and Archie Ronald—along with James Hunter and Hugh McEachran. With the exception of Archie McInnes, all were farmers. All were men of good will, though, naturally they could enjoy a gossip in congenial company.

Hugh McEachran, gruff, honest, red-bearded like Isaac in the Old Testament, perhaps exercised a greater influence on the Padre than did any of the others. (If Isaac's beard wasn't red it ought to have been.) He lived on a neighbouring farm and they met every day. To us boys he seemed deserving of unusual respect because he always spoke his mind, was never 'gushing' in his relations with children and often used the word 'bloody' without knowing it. Once, to our secret joy, we heard him introduce it twice into a short conversation with the Duchess.

In *Salt in My Porridge* I quoted his dying words to my father, and I make no excuse for quoting them again, because to me they contain the ultimate tribute to the Christian faith. When asked if he wasn't afraid to die, Hugh smiled and shook his head. 'Feart, minister?' he whispered. 'Why should I be feart?'

In 1971 I was asked by Dr William Morris to speak in Glasgow Cathedral. It was an unexpected invitation, which I accepted not because I felt adequate—far from it—but because my parents, had they been alive, would have encouraged me to do so. I had no idea what I ought to talk about in such awesome surroundings, but in the end I told the congregation about Old Hugh. His was a simple, earthy faith, and it is on such that even great cathedrals are built.

For many years he was kirk treasurer in Southend. Now the treasurer is his nephew, Robert Kelly, whose appointment to the post afforded the Padre great pleasure. My father also lived to see the ordination to the session of Archie MacKay's son, another Archie, and of Archie Ronald's son, John. Archie McCorkindale's nephew, John of that ilk, though not an elder, is a member of the Congregational Board.

A few years ago, for some odd reason, the congregation voted me into the eldership. At first I refused the call, because I felt unworthy. This was no outburst of mock modesty. Like the Padre, I believe I'm able to look all my shortcomings in the face. In the end, however, I accepted it, because my mother had an idea it might improve my character. Grannie, as we called her in later years, had an enduring and sometimes unreasoning faith in her husband and family. She was, essentially, far more a Christian than any of us, including my father. I loved her and became an elder to make her happy, though she died before the ordination took place.

The session of Southend Parish Church in 1974 has, therefore, many ties of blood and of ethos with that of 1924. As in another business, the show goes on. A tradition is maintained. A new faith, still crude but perhaps becoming more and more infused with love, is built on the foundation of the old.

Archie MacKay tenanted the farm of Lephinstrath. He had a white beard, deep-sunk twinkling eyes and a handshake that hurt our fingers but was somehow reassuring. His standards of belief were never intolerant or unmindful of human failings; but the stories he told after supper at the Manse often had a moral.

He was extremely proud of his encounter, just after World War I, with two young midshipmen. Their ship was anchored in Campbeltown Loch. On a visit to the lighthouse at the Mull of Kintyre, three miles further on through the hills, they left their hired car at Lephinstrath and completed the journey on foot. When they returned, Archie invited them into his house to drink glasses of milk and eat platefuls of soda scones spread with home-made strawberry jam. One of them, a most attractive personality, was loud in his praise of the strawberry jam. Days later Archie discovered who he was: Prince George, the Duke of Kent.

There used to be a treasured photograph on the mantelpiece at Lephinstrath. It was of the two midshipmen sitting together in their bone-shaker car.

One night at the Manse Archie told a story which is a limpet on my memory. Its authenticity is confirmed by the kirk records; but I have never used it as a plot for fiction because I suspect no editor or producer would give it credence. A Shakespeare might be able to turn the trick; not a MacVicar.

It concerned a young couple who lived in Southend at the beginning of last century. Their names were Angus MacMath and Helen MacKay. (Helen was Archie's own great grand aunt.) They fell in love, got married and were happy working their croft.

On a summer evening, about a year after the wedding, Angus went fishing for lithe and *gleaseans* in the Sound of Sanda, with three friends. It was beginning to get dark, and they were about to go home, when suddenly a fast frigate bore down on them. Too late they realised they'd been caught by the press-gang.

The two older men were allowed freedom, but Angus and his

friend, John McMurchy, were taken for service in the Navy.

For eighteen months Angus wrote to his Helen with surprising regularity. His letters were cheerful and looked forward to a speedy homecoming. Then the letters stopped.

Three years later, John McMurchy returned to Southend, discharged after serving his time. He told of a naval engagement with the French in the West Indies and how he himself had escaped with his life while Angus was posted missing. Helen wept and tried desperately to remain hopeful.

The years went past. A middle-aged bachelor, a ploughman on a neighbouring farm called David Reid, often helped Helen with the croft, and eventually he asked her to marry him. At first reluctant, in the end she approached the kirk session for advice. As nothing had been heard of Angus for seven years the minister and elders came to the conclusion that he must be dead. In the circumstances they saw no impediment, religious or legal, to her marrying David Reid.

The wedding took place, and David went to live with Helen on the croft.

Not long afterwards, as David and Helen sat by the fire on a winter's night, a knock came to the door. It was Angus, back from the wars. He told them how he'd been taken prisoner by the French and released only a week or two before.

Helen found courage and explained to him about David.

Recovering from the shock, Angus finally suggested a solution. He would go out by the west door of the crofthouse. David Reid would go out by the east door, and Helen would call back the man she wanted. . . .

At this point the storyteller paused, looking across at Archie, Willie and me. He would have been a good producer of amateur drama. 'Well,' he said, 'which one do you think she called after?'

We shook our heads.

'She called to Angus,' he told us. 'And when you grow up and understand the ladies—like your father—you'll know why.'

'But what about David Reid?' we asked, immediately sad on account of the underdog.

'He left the parish that night,' said Archie, 'and he never came back. He was a good man, you see, with a sense of what is right.'

This is a true story. It happened just as Archie MacKay said. But even then my brothers and I couldn't help wondering if life always resolves itself in terms of such simple black and white.

Archie McInnes was the local shoemaker, lean, clean-shaven, with high cheekbones. He was a bachelor, living with his sister in a small house in the village. The low-ceilinged kitchen was his shop. When we went with boots or shoes to mend we would sit by the glowing steel range watching him with fascination as on his stool by the window he attached a new sole to a working boot. The giant 'needle' (or awl) would flash, the little hammer would crack down, he'd spit on his hand and in a second the waxed twine would be in place, forming another stitch in the welt. It was all done so quickly and in such a professional way that we could scarcely follow his movements.

At work he wore a leather apron and steel-rimmed spectacles. In his leisure time inclined to be a dandy, he favoured grey worsted suits, the jackets buttoning tightly from breastbone to pelvis, stiff white collars and gaudy ties kept in place by a silver clasp. His grey hair was plentifully treated with some kind of unguent (cobbler's wax?) and combed into a cylindrical shape from forehead to crown.

When he performed his duty as an elder at communion, helping to serve a hushed congregation with the bread and wine, he was a memorable sight, clad in a black frock coat, grey tweed trousers and a gleaming stiff white shirt and collar, with an equally stiff and white bow tie. Fifty years ago this was the customary attire of an elder in Southend Parish Church. But Archie's clothes were never rumpled or stained as some of the farmers' were.

Maimie frequently spent a social evening with Archie and his sister Katie. At one time I had a notion that she and Archie might make a match of it. The thought was dire, because life at the Manse without Maimie would have been unsupportable. When I mentioned it to my brothers their jealous reaction was immediate. In fact Willie burst into tears and informed Maimie that if she married 'that rotten shoemaker' he himself would never love her again. Nothing came of the romance.

Archie was a charming, precisely fastidious old man, who saw good in everybody and never gossiped about his neighbours. To the ladies he was always gallant. While the other elders greeted my mother with rough shyness, he would bow over her hand like a courtier and address her in a flowery accent. The accent soon wore off, but his good manners never failed to impress us children.

They didn't impress his contemporaries. Indeed, some folk in the parish were inclined to regard Archie as a figure of fun. His image wasn't helped by a mincing gait which made his shoes appear too small for him. The trouble was he had bunions, which the long-striding farmers and shepherds of Southend looked upon as an effeminate weakness.

During World War I he became a member of Southend's contingent of the National Guard, the forerunner of *Dad's Army* in World War II. The village boys had a rhyme which they repeated *ad nauseam* in the school playground:

> The charge of the National Guard!
> Big Morton [the schoolmaster] led the charge!
> Archie Innes wi' the feet
> Was the first to retreat
> At the charge of the National Guard!

Even then I thought this was unfair. Archie McInnes, I felt sure, had the courage never to retreat. At any rate, he had the courage to be unorthodox in a highly orthodox community.

He was a first-class shoemaker. The leather he used was of the best, his own work always that of a painstaking craftsman. It was said he had money, and it may well be that through the years, living frugally with a capable sister as housekeeper, he had been able to save a little. Certainly in matters of dress he didn't stint himself. But I have an idea he lived on a narrow margin like everybody else in the parish and that his life-style, like his expert work as a shoemaker, was simply a thumb-to-nose flourish against fate.

He taught in the Sunday School. As a religious instructor he was 'gey dreich', but sometimes he made up for it by telling us cautionary tales about black savages in Africa. Their terrible cannibalistic practices, as he described them, made us shiver. The source of his information about the 'darkies', as he called them, I have never been able to discover. But he had a relative who worked as a missionary in the Congo.

He had a strange custom, on the last day of Sunday School, of making us read the fifth chapter of Genesis. Like drugged zombies we ploughed our way through the 'begats', our tongues tripping on names like Mahalaleel and Jared, our minds boggling at the information that at the age of 187 Methuselah had found strength to beget Lamech and that, thereafter, he had gone on happily begetting more and more sons and daughters for 782 years. '*And all the days of Methuselah were nine hundred sixty and nine years: and he died.*' No wonder he died, we thought: he must have been exhausted.

If Archie had heard that the years of Methuselah were possibly months in modern reckoning—or that, alternatively, Methuselah was the name of a tribe— he never told us. He offered us the Bible straight, and for this reason, as pragmatic children, it was a long time before we gave it any serious consideration.

Nevertheless, we were prepared to admit that it did contain a few 'super' yarns, like the one about Samson. I forestalled Cecil B. de Mille by several decades and, at the age of ten, wrote an epic play about the destruction of the temple. We acted it out in the Manse back yard, with my brother Archie as Samson. The wall of an outhouse, deliberately undermined, fell down on top of him, and I injured my ankle while essaying a parachute drop from the outhouse roof. The parachute was my father's funeral umbrella. I was playing God.

In general, however, the Bible stories interested us a great deal less than the extravagant yarns which old Archie McInnes himself was in the habit of telling. They were, perhaps, another reason why some people in Southend gave him less solid respect than he deserved. But for us—and especially for me, with the writing bug already in my veins—they were spell-binding.

One supper evening at the Manse, principally for the benefit of my brothers and myself, I think, he recited the famous local tale of Big Hamish of the Terrible Fingers. No Hitchcock film ever stirred us more.

He prepared the ground by telling us that in the eighteenth century Southend was an ideal landing-place for contraband. Its coast was wild and deserted, and on their journey through the North Channel to the Clyde the West Indian merchant ships, from whom smugglers bought their cargoes, sailed close to the shore. Moreover, the smugglers were mostly fishermen by trade, and their intimate knowledge of the tides in the area often enabled them to avoid capture by the revenue men.

Revenue cutters made their appearance in the Firth of Clyde soon after 1745. At first the task-force was small; but towards the end of the century the amount of rum and tobacco sold throughout Scotland by the Kintyre smugglers had become so great that a naval station was established in Campbeltown, and a fleet of cutters began a constant patrol between the Mull of Kintyre and the Mull of Galloway.

After this the smuggling skippers had to go warily. Some were caught red-handed, the fiery Jamaican rum in their holds and in the stomachs of their crews. For a period they would disappear. When they returned from the penal settlements in the West Indies, bodies bloodless and dry from long exposure to the sun, their taste for adventure would have changed to one for the fireside.

Hamish MacDonald, however, the most notorious of the Kintyre smugglers, continued to be a thorn in the side of the Government. His two-masted, lug-sailed vessel—somewhat larger than a modern m.f.v., but not unlike it in build—was nearly as fast as the cutters. He chose his crew for their ability to keep their counsel as well as for their seamanship. Though under suspicion, he remained a free man, with a store of gusty laughter in his red beard for the fruitless efforts of the excisemen.

He was only of medium height, but his strength, Archie McInnes told us, was enormous. His hairy hands could grip like grappling irons. Once, in a fit of rage at an insult to his daughter, he performed a feat like that of Blackmore's 'girt John Ridd'. Seizing the throat of the girl's tormentor with one hand, he clutched the muscle of his upper arm with the other and tore it out as he might have stripped a bow of its string. . . .

My brothers and I shivered and thought: *No wonder he was called Big Hamish of the Terrible Fingers.*

In the records of the town of Campbeltown, according to old Archie's story, there is an entry to the effect that in 1785, or thereabouts, William Huskisson of Liverpool was appointed chief officer of excise in the district of Kintyre. This man proved himself hugely unpopular both with the natives and with those under his command. Two of the latter, Lieutenant Martin and Lieutenant Munro, were continually under the lash of his intolerance.

From the beginning, Huskisson was determined to put an end to Hamish MacDonald's activities. He incited the North Channel patrol to even greater vigilance. But in the first three months of his regime Hamish sailed a cargo of rum and tobacco from Northern Ireland to Southend without allowing the excisemen even a glimpse of his lugger, the *Diana*.

Huskisson raved and blasphemed. Martin and Munro, joint commanders of the patrol, were told that if by the end of the year MacDonald hadn't been brought before the sheriff at Campbeltown, they would be summarily dismissed the service. But Hamish carried on his trade unchecked, and it wasn't surprising that his surbordinates' hatred of Huskisson—and of the smuggler, too, as the indirect cause of their misfortunes—gradually became an obsession.

Huskisson lived in Macharioch House, in Southend. As a rule it was to this many-gabled mansion, later rebuilt by the Duke of Argyll for his Duchess, that Martin and Munro were summoned to receive instruction and criticism.

At one of these conferences, which took place about the beginning of winter, the two young officers outlined a scheme to their chief, suggesting that on the following Sunday he should invite MacDonald to Macharioch in a feigned spirit of friendliness. The three of them could then ply him with wine in the hope that careless bravado would lead him to betray the time of his next smuggling venture. After some bad-natured argument Huskisson agreed to the plan.

The difficulty was how to get Hamish to Macharioch. Clearly his suspicions would be aroused were he to receive a bald invitation to visit his arch-enemy. Further, though his exploits were known to them only too well, up to this time neither Huskisson nor his lieutenants had spoken to or even set eyes on the notorious smuggler.

Huskisson, however, solved the problem in a typically un-scrupulous way. To the cot-house under the Rock of Dunaverty he sent a letter, which, to this day, is preserved by Hamish's descendants. (Or so old Archie informed us.) This proposed a working agreement by which Hamish would receive from Huskisson himself a sum of money yearly in return for a cessation of his smuggling activities. In order to discuss the details the smuggler was invited to Macharioch.

Hamish had no inkling of guile. The tone of defeat in the letter appealed only to his sense of humour. He laughed hugely at the thought of Huskisson and his minions bending their wills to his. Next Sunday night found him seated in a high-backed chair of carved oak, facing the three excisemen across an open hearth.

The conversation was strained. Contrary to expectations, after a third glass Hamish refused all further offers of wine. He had seen through Huskisson's early efforts to pump him. In answering questions he had become wary as a hawk.

The others noticed, too, that since coming into the room he had kept his left hand buried deep in the wide side-pocket of his seaman's jacket. Had he a knife hidden there? Or a primed pistol?

Unlike their guest, Martin and Munro drank freely. As the night went on their faces became flushed, their speech thick. Martin, a big-muscled man, moved restlessly about the candle-lit room, knocking against the furniture.

Hamish tried to bring up the subject of the proposed agreement; but Huskisson hummed and hawed and at length showed signs of losing his temper.

Hamish suppressed anger, but his blue eyes were hot. Huskisson saw how once or twice that hidden left hand twitched inside the pocket as if his guest were fingering some deadly weapon. He was glad now he had taken his lieutenants' advice to have within the house an armed posse of sheriff's men.

It was almost midnight when Martin, during one of his uneasy tours of the room, stumbled against the table on which stood the fat, wax candles. Immediately the four men were in darkness.

A chill silence, then a horrible choking sound and a scuffling of feet, heavily booted.

The noises ceased.

'Light!' roared Martin.

With trembling hands Munro ignited a fuse and lifted the fallen candles. Hastily he lit them.

The sudden glow of light discovered Munro by the table, Martin slumped in a chair by the door and Hamish standing immobile in front of the hearth, his left hand still buried from sight in his pocket. Not three yards from his feet Huskisson lay dead on the floor, the livid marks of five biting fingers on his upturned throat.

Martin leapt to his feet. 'MacDonald,' he shouted, 'you have done this! I have heard about the strength of your fingers. Munro, bring them in!'

Munro called and five men, four of them armed with muskets, entered the room.

The florid-faced officer in charge stepped forward. He saw the body with its face grinning at the ceiling. He waited, apparently unmoved, for someone to speak.

More sober now, Martin explained. 'Huskisson has been murdered. A few minutes ago the candles went out. He was strangled in the dark.'

Stolidly the officer said: 'Who did it?'

'Hamish MacDonald! Who else? Big Hamish of the Terrible Fingers!'

'Wait!' The smuggler's voice was hard. 'I see the marks of five fingers on Huskisson's throat. Are they not all fingers of a left hand?'

The officer glanced down. 'That is the truth,' he said.

'Then I, for one,' said Hamish, 'am not guilty!'

For the first time that night he took his left hand from his pocket. No doubt the fear of betraying a weakness had made him keep it there.

Martin gasped when he saw it. The thing was a mass of pulpy red flesh, and the thumb and the first two fingers were missing. . . .

My brothers and I let out sighs of satisfaction. We noticed that some of the other elders were smiling among themselves and shaking their heads; but it didn't spoil our enjoyment of a magnificent climax.

Then, in a voice as precise as the set of his hair, Archie ('Hitchcock') McInnes dealt with the denouement. In due course Martin was found guilty of the murder, he said, with Munro sharing his punishment as an accessory before the fact. Their plan to rid themselves of both Huskisson and MacDonald at a stroke had been brilliant. It had failed because of their ignorance of one important fact. A few months before the excisemen came to Kintyre, during a stormy crossing from Cushendun in Northern Ireland to Southend, the smuggler's left hand had been caught in the rigging of the *Diana* and cruelly mangled.

While working on the *Campbeltown Courier* years later, I remembered this remarkable tale and tried to find Huskisson's name in the town records. I failed. Nor can I discover in Southend a descendant of the legendary smuggler who has a copy of the Judas letter.

Did old Archie concoct the whole thing out of his vivid imagination? Behind the dandified exterior did there lurk the soul of a desperate smuggler? I don't know the answers. But the plot of his story was so good—too good to be true?—that, in various forms, I have used it many times to earn a few quick guineas.

On those supper occasions there were other stories by other elders. Archie and Willie and I sat quiet and intent, enjoying the dramatic moments. Looking back, I am certain we inspired the old men to give of their best, in the same way as a new and sympathetic audience can sometimes inspire ageing actors to peak performances.

As the night grew old we would try to remain as inconspicuous as possible in case our parents might decide we weren't 'being good' and send us to bed. But the elders, I think, were always aware of us.

Archie McCaig would describe the great shinty matches which, in his boyhood, used to take place in Southend on New Year's Day. Teams from Connieglen and Glenbreckrie—the two wide valleys on either side of 'the hill' which are the populated parts of the parish—would meet on the open *machair*-land, belonging to

Gartvaigh Farm, which is called Strathmore. Sometimes each side would consist of as many as fifty men, and the battle would be fierce. I used to picture it as being like the great conflict on the Inch of Perth, between Clan Chattan and Clan Kay, which Mr Morton had told us about at school.

Then Archie McCaig would shake his head and mutter in his beard about the curse of drink. As times passed, he explained, the games got out of hand. They became more like drinking matches than shinty matches, and family feuds took root when men went home with broken hands and noses and reported attacks made on them by relatives and rivals.

Discipline was forgotten. It became fashionable to use the *caman* on an opponent rather than on the ball. The end came when one player was so badly injured by a blow on the head from a shinty-stick that in a few days he died.

It used to puzzle us that the elders—and my farther—should utter so many hard words against 'the drink' when most of the time, as they spoke, they were enjoying what my brother called 'a drop of spirits'. Eventually we came to the conclusion that the evil wasn't so much in the drink itself as in the way it was used.

Hugh McEachran had a story of treasure hidden on his farm of Kilblaan. After Culloden, he said, a Jacobite soldier, dodging the Hanoverian redcoats, fled to Kintyre. Somewhere, during his wanderings, he stole a sackload of gold and silver candlesticks from a deserted house. Before embarking in the Black Wherry, which would take him from Southend to the comparative safety of Ireland, he buried his loot under the bank of a stream about half-a-mile north of Kilblaan farmhouse. The soldier never returned, and the treasure, Hugh assured us, was still there.

We goggled at him. Could he tell us exactly where the place was?

'Come ower tae the bloody ferm the morn. I'll show ye.'

He kept his word. With our seashore pails and spades we dug there feverishly on many a cold day after school. But we found nothing.

I reckon we didn't dig deep enough or at exactly the right spot. If any modern treasure hunter fancies his chances I should be glad to show him the place old Hugh showed us. It *looks* promising. It always did look promising. . . .

An evening with the elders was something we anticipated with delight. The winter nights were long. There was no radio, no television. Outside the Manse were no street lamps: when the moon was down we faced only a blanket of dark and a moaning in the trees. So we stayed inside, avoiding ghostly terrors. Children's books were too expensive for clerical pockets, and, except when the Duchess brought some up-to-date annuals, we had to rely for reading excitement on my father's favourite, Sir Walter Scott. The stories told by the elders were down-to-earth, unsophisticated, personalised, much more to our taste.

I was going to be a storyteller myself. To the old masters on the Kirk Session I owe a debt 'as deep as a well'.

5

Dancing Years

Soon after World War I, when I was eleven, summer dancing classes were inaugurated in Southend by Mr McLeish. He was an elderly man with a blue and red complexion and a large moustache with waxed points. His legs being stiff with rheumatism, he was less mobile than our preconceived image of a dancing master; but he had a referee's whistle which he used loudly and often to keep pupils in order. He had an irascible and sometimes forbidding manner.

His assistant was a charming young lady with a cloche hat, who may might have been his daughter. She had beautiful legs and danced like an angel. Her piano playing was superb.

When I went to the University in Glasgow, in 1926, I found a dance hall near Charing Cross with the legend *McLeish's School of Dancing* in gold letters above the door. It would seem, therefore, that Mr McLeish had a shrewd head for business. When his city school closed for the summer he went on tour in the country and earned enough to give his daughter and himself a tonic change of air for free.

His class in Southend was advertised as being for children from nine to fourteen. Archie and Willie, therefore, were too young to go, and Rona was only a baby; but, much against my will, I was enrolled in it by parents who judged I might benefit by a wider knowledge of the social graces. Each Saturday afternoon I trudged down the road to the Territorial Hall, where the class was held, envying my brothers and their friends playing football in the glebe or bathing in the Minister's Lynn.

Some of the lads from the village, encountering me dressed to kill and carrying my pumps, gave me the horse-laugh. I was humiliated. Dancing, I thought: a pastime for girls, and here was I forced to endure it. Only the background picture of a father skilled in the use of a hair-brush, and a mother liable to sad eyes if I disappointed her, kept me in the narrow way.

At first Mr McLeish did his best to carve a dancer out of recalcitrant teak. But my legs were long, my feet clumsy, my body as ungainly as a foal's. I could run faster than any of my friends, but agility forsook me when I essayed a *pas de bas* or a light turn on my toes. There may have been a psychological as well as a physical blockage. It was rooted in my mind that dancing was for cissies. As a result I could never bring myself to enjoy it or to relax sufficiently to execute an intricate pattern of steps. Finally, and inevitably, Mr McLeish gave up the struggle.

When the class came to an end in August, his pupils were presented to parents and friends in a Grand Display of Dancing. Among the audience, smiling graciously, was the Dowager Duchess. So were a number of my school mates, cat-calling from the back of the hall. Thankfully, however, I had been relegated by this time to comparative obscurity. My only part in the Display —except for an appearance in the opening grand march, which wasn't so bad because my tiny partner kept me right—was to act as a statue in the statue dance. This entailed standing rock-still for about ten minutes, one arm outstretched, the other akimbo, while dainty girls, light as gossamer, danced around me. I suffered in sullen gloom, while the cat-calls from the back became an uproar and Archie and Willie, with my mother in the front row, stifled their giggles behind toffee-stained fingers.

(I seem to remember that Boskers was another statue. One of these days, when we're playing golf, I must ask him.)

But good, as they say, often comes out of evil. My partner for the Grand March was Jean Smith McKerral, the nine-year-old daughter of the tenant farmer in Brunerican. She was small and, as a rule, shy. But when the music began she became a different creature, eyes sparkling, legs twinkling, able to pirouette like a ballet star. To have been chosen as partner for a lout like me must have been disappointing for her, but she did her duty without demur and in the end steered me successfully through the intricacies of the grand march.

She was the youngest of a family of eight, the first seven of which were boys, so I expect that dealing with one more incompetent male was less of a problem for her than it might have been for many other girls.

That afternoon she did her best to cheer my drooping spirits. She has been doing it ever since.

Sixteen years later we married. Fifty-four years later we're still together. She dances as lightly and gaily as ever. When I venture on the floor I perform like a cart-horse. Or a statue.

The McKerrals have been in Brunerican for about two hundred years. The farm is now owned by Jean's nephew, Donnie, who has a healthy young family of three boys and a girl. It looks, therefore, as if the McKerrals may be there for another two hundred years, provided the Common Market doesn't put a spanner in the agricultural works.

The first remembered McKerral crossed from Ireland to Southend in the late sixteenth century. His native township was Ballytioram on the Antrim coast, north of the valley of Glendun. He spelt his name Maolgirg. Later the suffix 'an' was added and the name became McKiergan, which means servant of St Ciric. The present form, McKerral, has probably been derived by phonetic change or by somebody confusing St Ciric with another saint called Caireall. About the middle of the seventeenth century the direct progenitor of the Brunerican McKerrals was Godfrey ('Gorrie Gow'), armourer to the MacDonalds of Kintyre. Later he set up on his own as a blacksmith and built a smithy on land now included in the farm of High Cattadale. As an example of the intricate coils of history in a community like Southend, I should add that Donnie McKerral's wife, Catherine, is a sister of the present owner of High Cattadale.

When Jean was only fourteen her mother died, and from that time she became the lady of the house at Brunerican, looking after her father, Willie McKerral, and the several brothers who still remained on the farm. She had the help of servants, of course, but still had to get up for the milking at five o'clock in the morning and see the same process through again in the late afternoon.

We saw each other in the evenings. Sometimes I left Brunerican for home long after midnight, and Jean was left with a ration of four hours' sleep. That, she says, is why she never grew higher than my breast-bone.

While I was a student in Glasgow we wrote long letters to each other twice a week. Afterwards, during my spell as office-boy *cum* reporter *cum* editor on the *Campbeltown Courier*, we were able to meet more often. But she had her duty to do by her father and brothers, and I had no money. Marriage was a mirage, floating farther and farther away into the distance.

I must have been a highly unsatisfactory boy-friend, commuting in and out of Southend at irregular intervals, alternately full of despondency and wild optimism, unable to buy her anything but the cheapest presents, of a jealous and possessive nature and, when we did go to a dance together, acting like a clod-hopper. (Come to think of it, exactly the same things can be said of me today.)

I did write 'poems' for her. She tells me this is what kept her interested, but I don't believe her. She was just naturally loyal and patient, and it was a good thing she had—and has—the solace of her music.

A love and appreciation of music is, I believe, one of the human characteristics which can be proved to be hereditary. Jean's forbears, including her father, her brothers, her nieces and nephews and our son, Jock, all have perfectly attuned ears for music. Jock plays the accordion, Jean plays the piano, both solo and as an accompanist. She plays for the Woman's Guild, for the WRI, for concerts and children's parties. Twenty years ago she was in bed for weeks with a slipped disc. On her feet at last, she felt weak and uncoordinated. She wept on my shoulder and said: 'Just think! I may never be able to play the piano again!' But she did, of course. And as beautifully as before.

In 1933 my first novel was published: *The Purple Rock*. I left the *Courier* and became a freelance writer, 'living on my wits' as kind friends put it. By this time I had a few pounds in the bank and Jean and I decided to buy an engagement ring. This meant I had to ask her father for her hand in marriage.

In his younger days, when organs were sinful in the sight of the

Lord, Willie McKerral had been precentor in the church choir. He took the weekly practices on a Friday night, banging his tuning-fork on the edge of a pew and leading his companions in dignified renderings of the old psalm tunes. And, since it was a weekday and therefore not holy, he took care never to use, while practising, the sacred words that would accompany the tunes on the Sabbath. This meant he had to find secular words to fit the music.

Once, in a confidential mood, he recited for my benefit the verse he used in practising Tune French.

> As I went ower by old Kilblaan
> I fell amang the whins.
> They scrabbit a' my face an' hauns
> An' ne'er forgot my shins.

In his own kitchen at Brunerican he had a modulator on the wall with which, at mealtimes, he tested the musical ability of his sons—and daughter.

Now he was in his late seventies, well built and tall, with a grey Van Dyke beard. He had only one arm. The other had been caught in the driving-belt of a threshing machine and subsequently amputated above the elbow. His stoic behaviour at the time of the accident was incredible. Consciousness never left him, and it was a long time before the doctor came with an injection. Yet not once, though he was over 60 at the time, did he utter a sound of pain or distress. The day after the operation he was sitting up in bed, smiling, asking the nurses for a plate of porridge and his pipe.

He loved a party with music and often conducted the revels with the stump of his arm. Jean attended to him faithfully, helping him dress and undress, cutting up his food at mealtimes, slicing his tobacco and filling and lighting his pipe a score of times each day.

He knew, or course, that I was courting his daughter. He liked us to come into his room for a chat and a 'wee cup of tea'. Then, about nine o'clock, he would leave us and go to bed. From him, as from the elders, I learned book-loads of Southend history.

In times past, it seems, there was an illicit still on Brunerican, and he had some chuckling stories concerning the presence of

mind of his great-grandmother in hoodwinking the excisemen, or
'gadgers' as he called them. Once, on seeing them riding towards
the house, she quickly concealed the bottles of 'hooch' among the
butter she was making. Their vain search completed, she offered
them a draught of buttermilk straight from the churn. They
described the drink as 'most refreshing'.

On another occasion the 'gadgers' searched the whole building
from attic to dairy and, as usual, found nothing.

When they'd gone her husband and family emerged from their
hiding-places. 'What on earth did you do with the stuff this time?'
they asked.

'I poured it into the pots under the beds. Gentlemen would
never look there!'

When old Willie told me this one, his eyes streamed with
laughter.

But there wasn't much laughter, to begin with at any rate, on
the evening I came to ask him for Jean.

It had been arranged that when the 'wee cup of tea' was finished
she should disappear to the kitchen with the cups and saucers. As
soon as her father and I were alone together I would broach the
subject.

It was an evening of strain. Old Willie must have had an inkling
of what lay in the wind, because he was unusually silent as he
drank his tea and started puffing his bed-time pipe. When Jean
left the room, so nervous that the china clattered on the tray, the
silence became even more ominous. I prayed for strength.

'Grand weather we're having,' I said.

'Ay. Oh, ay. A bit drouthy for the turnips.'

'But good for the hay.'

'Ay. Good for the hay.' He coughed like an amateur actor,
inspected the bowl of his pipe, swallowed once or twice and
added: 'But bad for the corn.'

'Oh, ay. Bad for the corn.'

'Late harvest,' he said.

'Late harvest,' I said.

There was a clock on the mantelpiece. It had a tick like a bomb.
He looked up, met my eyes. He said: 'You're no' a singer?'

'A what?'

'A singer. You're no' a singer?'

'No, no. I'm not a singer. Not like Jean. Or the boys.'

'But you're a golfer?'

'Oh, ay. I'm a golfer!'

'It takes all sorts,' he said.

The situation was becoming desperate. I don't think either of us knew exactly what we were saying. I heard a movement in the passage outside and guessed that Jean had finished washing the cups and saucers and was now listening behind the door.

'Mr McKerral!' I said.

The stump of arm jerked. He sat upright in his chair. 'Ay? What is it?'

'There's something,' I said.

He sighed and looked troubled.

Then, like a dam bursting, I got it out. 'Have I your permission to give Jean an engagement ring and marry her?'

He blew through his pipe. Sparks flared up from the bowl. 'A ring?'

'Ay, a ring.'

'Ay, well—but don't get married yet. Wait a wee while.'

'Oh, sure, sure!' I was exhausted with relief.

He laughed, waved the moment aside with his pipe. 'Did I ever tell you the time my great-granny hid the stuff in the field behind the house and forgot where she put it?'

Jean came in. The ordeal, for all three of us, was over.

A few months later the old man took ill. He died as he had lived, stoically and without complaint.

Jean and I were married the following year, on 24 June 1936.

Pooling our meagre resources, and aided by a loan from a kindly County Council, we built a bungalow on the shore at Southend, a mile and a half from the Manse. We called it Achnamara, which means 'field of the sea'.

The only monetary investment we have ever made, except for insurance, it has turned out to be a good one. For the house, a substantial garage and a concrete wall guarding our precious

quarter acre, the bill was exactly £1000. Today we could sell it
for more than £10,000. But this is irrelevant. We wouldn't sell
it for £100,000. It will be our one and only legacy to Jock (apart
from a few declining royalties from books and plays), and I
know he will appreciate having 'a wee house in the country' when
he decides to retire from sports reporting with the *Daily Express*.

Over the years Achnamara has acquired a new, gale-proof porch,
a more efficient heating system and double-glazed windows. But
we still use the desk my parents gave us when we married. We still
sit in the armchairs which were gifts from Archie and Willie.
These chairs, deep caverns of comfort after a game of golf or a
day's work in the garden, cost £5 each in 1936. In a magazine the
other day I saw an advertisement for one not quite so comfortable
but similar in other respects. Its price? £130.

Jean and I are not clever about money. We wanted enough to
be able to live in reasonable comfort and, when Jock arrived in
1937, a little extra to give him a start in life. But a writer's income
always fluctuates violently, according to circumstances, from perhaps £100 in one week to zero in the next three, and our married
life, therefore, has seldom been without financial anxieties. This
has made us consider carefully our situation from year to year,
and worry-laden analyses reveal the fact that in 1971, when my
gross income was about £2000, we were no more affluent than in
1937, when it was £350. Now, in 1974, I reckon I should have to
earn at least £3000 in order to maintain our standard of living.
For an author without trade union backing, living under a system
which compels him to work for nothing on behalf of library
customers who read his books for free, without the aid of grants
or subsidies, this kind of income is attainable only by a miracle.

Inflation may burn like a bonfire, but never mind. The sea outside the front windows of Achnamara is restless, blue and full of
interest, especially in a storm. The grass in the fields is green, and
whins blaze yellow on the raised beaches behind the house. The
vegetables in the garden are fresh, non-plastic. The swallows build
their nests in the garage and under the eaves. In winter a robin
comes to peck at Jean's crocuses. The air is clean. Except in summer
when the visitors arrive, cars, buses and lorries pass on the road at

the rate of about half-a-dozen an hour. There's the kirk and the golf and the amateur drama and the pub, and our neighbours are kind. And—Beveridge be blessed!—there's always the Old Age Pension. . . .

In 1936, when we set up house, we bought a blue second-hand Morris Oxford, 14 h.p., for £30. Jean didn't smoke, but I did, and the packet of 20 Capstan which soothed my long wrestlings with words cost 11½d.

We had an imposing 'wireless', two feet tall and eighteen inches wide, a wedding present from Jean's eldest brother, James. We listened in the evenings to bands conducted by Henry Hall, Primo Scala and Roy Fox. When they played *Smoke Gets in Your Eyes* I was almost inclined to dance. We were moved by the broadcast describing the death of King George V and later caught up in the excitement and argument surrounding the abdication. The BBC did masterly work on both. I believe it was better then at reflecting the views and sensibilities of the listening majority than it is today.

Our wireless was powered by an enormous battery (or was accumulator the technical term?), which had to be recharged at monthly intervals. When sated with Henry Hall and Arthur Askey, we switched off and read our newspapers (1d each) and our paper-backs (6d each) by the light of paraffin lamps.

At that time we had no electricity in Southend. We remained without it until 1950; and I remember, during the war, how surprised I was to discover that every hilltop village in Italy was ablaze with bulbs.

As in Italy, the remote parts of Scotland are damp with the foam of a thousand waterfalls, yet not until after the war did anybody in Edinburgh or London put into serious practice the idea of harnessing their power. There was plenty of light on Princes Street and in Piccadilly, so I expect nobody worried much about the folk with heather in their ears. (That is, until the war came. Then we were encouraged to join our great and glorious Highland regiments and given every facility to die for our great and glorious government.)

I buy quantities of 'copy' paper for my work and enjoy an

occasional visit from the representative of a London-based paper firm. With headquarters in Glasgow, he travels throughout the West of Scotland by car. He told me that his firm had at first decided to station him in Rothesay, until somebody in the office, producing a map, pointed out that Rothesay was on an island and that instead of a car the representative would need a helicopter.

This story reminds me of a Gaelic legend. When God finished making Britain, some fragments of earth and stone were left in his ample apron. With a smile he flicked them out, and they fell into the western sea to form Argyll and the Isles. A more modern legend, obviously unknown to the directorate of the London paper firm, declares that the coastline of Argyll and Bute alone, tortuously wriggling among islands and sea-lochs, stretches for 3000 miles.

The roads also wriggle tortuously, with the result, for example, that a journey from Southend to Ayr, 40 miles for a crow, is 187 for a motorist groping wearily around Loch Fyne, Loch Long and almost the entire Firth of Clyde. Car owners in Mull, Islay and other islands have problems that are even worse.

Here is a situation which ought, surely, to be considered urgently and in an imaginative way. For decades Ministers of Power ignored the need for electricity in the Highlands. Should present-day Ministers of Transport be branded as equally slow and unimaginative? They have the example of Norway. Its coastline is toothy and indented like that of Argyll and the Isles, but every fiord is served by an efficient car-ferry, and the scheme is run on a national basis. Scotland's Western Ferries have an idea of what is wanted, but politics have bedevilled their tentative operations between Kintyre and Islay and Kintyre and Northern Ireland, and for any motorist—except a meandering holidaymaker—the West Coast of Scotland remains a tarmac nightmare of twists and turns and long, unnecessary hours at the wheel.

Have I fallen into the common trap of expecting ideas always to be translated speedily into action? Speed, after all, is relative.

When we lived in Achnamara at first, Jean and I had two delightful neighbours, Mrs Robertson and Mrs MacSporran. (There *is* a name MacSporran: it belongs to Kintyre. And, believe it or not, there are people called MacHaggis in the South of Scotland.) Both were widows in their eighties, living alone on their pensions. Both had given birth to large families and were now content and happy to lead a quieter life. They were full of humour. We always referred to them as 'the Keil dowagers', and they laughed about it and put on an act for our benefit.

On a Sunday, when we picked them up in the old Morris to take them to church, they'd often appear in old-fashioned gowns of black crepe decorated with strings of beads. The gowns were ample and flowing and required much tucking-in as their wearers settled themselves in the back seat of the car. Mrs Robertson would accept such ministrations with a slightly haughty air, Mrs MacSporran with a twinkle in her bright eye.

'We're that grand,' Mrs MacSporran remarked one Sunday, 'you'd think we had meal to sell!' (Which is a saying we use in Southend when referring to folk who act above their financial station.)

But the point I'm trying to make is this. Both old ladies were born into poor homes, where the only source of light in winter was a *cruiskan*, a saucer-shaped oil-holder fitted with a wick of twine and tallow. But in eighty years they saw the *cruiskan* become a candle, a candle a paraffin lamp, a paraffin lamp a pressure lamp and a pressure lamp an electric bulb, clean and easy.

Does progress appear to be sluggish only because we all have so meagre a ration of time on this old earth?

In the first three years of our married life, Jean and I listened to Roy Fox playing 'There's a good time coming, be it ever so far away'. We had Jock, a house of our own, an income which showed signs of increasing and the opportunity of enjoying plenty of fresh air and exercise. We weren't thinking about good times to come. We had them.

Then one Sunday morning, at eleven o'clock, Chamberlain's emasculated voice came from the loudspeaker of our wireless, announcing that war had begun. The times became less good.

I was a member of the evacuation committee and spent unhappy days trying to find accommodation in Southend for mothers and children from Glasgow. When the evacuees did come, Achnamara was filled with rushing, talking people, old and young, and Jean wept when a child smashed the glass of a display cabinet.

But in less than a week most of the families returned to Glasgow. Southend had no cinema, no café, few amenities of an urban kind. To women used to cooking by electricity or by gas our paraffin stoves must have appeared like relics from the stone age. To children in the habit of roaming the lamplit streets the darkness of a night in Southend, filled with the ominous grumble of sea-waves, must have been daunting. By the end of September, 1939, no adults and only a few children remained in the parish.

During all this time I had been feeling out of sorts. I became thin and pale, and Jean and Jock must have suffered because of my irritation. I shivered in the evenings and felt tired and dizzy when morning came. I tried to keep on writing, but there was no spark, no power of concentration. Even golf became unattractive. Meanwhile the war was dragging on and our small savings were dwindling away. I had a premonition of defeat.

In December I became so ill that I had to stay in bed. A local doctor told Jean—not in my hearing—that he suspected galloping consumption. I was flown by air-ambulance to a nursing-home in Glasgow.

There I was X-rayed and found *not* to be suffering from tuberculosis. I was put on a course of pills which contained arsenic. In eleven weeks I was cured.

In *Salt in My Porridge* I described my experience in the nursing-home and told how the doctor in charge diagnosed an Eastern disease, the name and nature of which he never divulged. Admitting that I am a bore on the subject of 'my illness', I also mentioned another doctor's theory that it might have been brucellosis.

Soon after *Salt in My Porridge* was published in 1971, I received the following letter:

> Dear Angus, Excuse the familiarity, but I have thought and talked of you as such for the past 31 years. Many medical students have been told of your illness in 1939–40 and also many of my colleagues. The rest of this letter will tell you why, because you don't seem to know yourself.

Recently I was given a party by my twin daughters for my eightieth birthday. One of my presents was *Salt in My Porridge*, and as most of the guests were doctors and nurses who had been on my staff at the Royal Infirmary (Glasgow), I told them the story of Angus MacVicar's illness. On reading your very enjoyable book a few days later I found it contained the story of your illness and was surprised that you evidently were not told what you had been suffering from. I will now tell you.

Reluctantly, after some weeks, your doctor in the nursing-home decided to consult a specialist. I was asked, because I was a consultant physician specialising in gastro-enterology, with wards in the Royal Infirmary. It was I who asked about whether you had any contact with foreigners, foreign ships, etc., and found that in August 1939, on your brother's ship, you had partaken of a salad prepared by a lascar. This gave me a clue at once and I had a specimen of faeces taken. I examined a portion myself and for corroboration had a specimen examined by the bacteriologist at the Royal Infirmary. My suspicion that you had amoebic dysentery was confirmed by finding cysts and live amoebae in the faeces, and this was confirmed by the bacteriologist.

Treatment was now straightforward and you were given Emetine Bismuth Iodide and Yatren and the condition responded very quickly, leaving you pretty washed out for a time. The memorable night after the injection (referred to in *Salt in My Porridge*) was due, if my memory is right, to Omnopon, which is a morphine derivative.

You can tell your friends now that you had amoebic dysentery and your doctor friend that it was not brucellosis.

The doctor in charge at the nursing-home should have told you the diagnosis, as you were his patient really. He was also going to write to your own doctor in Southend and said that I need not write.

My notes on your case were destroyed a few years after I retired in 1956, but 'Angus MacVicar's Amoebic Dysentery' is known to many, but evidently not to yourself. Your case history is quite unique.

With best wishes now and always. Your sincerely, David Smith.

Dr Smith lives in Bearsden, near Glasgow. I was thrilled to receive his letter. For nearly a quarter of a century I had been completely unaware that my name occurred among his long list of patients. I'm glad I wrote *Salt in My Porridge*. Otherwise I should never have been able to thank this distinguished, precise and characteristically modest physician for saving my life.

Jean adds her word to that.

(And now I'll be a bigger bore than ever about 'my illness'.)

6

Certain Fountains of Justice

I gave up the idea of becoming a minister ostensibly because of a bad stammer. A more important reason may have been that I hadn't the courage to tackle one of the most difficult jobs on earth. But perhaps the real reason was that I had my heart set on becoming a writer.

In 1931, five years before Jean and I got married, I said goodbye to the University and looked around for a job: preferably a job to do with writing. With 2,000,000 unemployed in the country, I was lucky to get one on the *Campbeltown Courier*, at £3 a week.

At the University I had come to understand how sheltered and secure our lives had been in a country manse. I found that the values and standards exemplified by our parents were not universal. A knowledge of the hard injustices some people had to endure because of selfishness and lack of neighbourly concern made me angry. Now, as a reporter with the *Courier*, I came in contact again with human distress, and my anger at those in positions of power and privilege who turned a blind eye to it became even stronger.

Alec MacLeod, the editor, was a superb journalist, with much humour in his writing. At times he himself would lambast the Establishment, but he discouraged my juvenile essays in 'bolshieness'. 'Destructive writing is easy,' he used to tell me. 'A good writer is always constructive.'

I worked on the *Courier* for about two years. During that time Alec was often unwell, and for periods I was left in charge of the paper. I enjoyed the feeling of responsibility this gave me. I enjoyed the altercations with people, mainly town councillors, who declared they were being wrongly reported. The family penchant for preaching and teaching was given full scope.

I had the willing guidance of the printers, all of them tough, independent characters, who, I think, sympathised with my brash ambition to record the truth and be fair to the underdog.

The head printer was Sandy McMurchy, stout and tall, who could speak, chew tobacco and hold half a dozen specimens of type in his mouth, all at the same time. An expert in the old-fashioned craft of hand-setting, he spent most of his working hours at the angled cases, composing 'copy' and advertisements for the paper in sticks of various sizes, and then, after use, 'dissing' the type back into the appropriate compartments in the cases. A slow and laborious job which lasted, for him, six and a half days a week.

He had two men under him. Arthur Henderson, pale and stocky, was skilled in general printing. He worked hard, said little and occupied, in his spare time, an important position in the local Masonic Lodge. Archie MacMillan, lean, grizzled and another inveterate chewer of tobacco, operated the linotype machine.

I remember a visit we had one afternoon from a factory inspector who, to our surprise, turned out to be a woman. She was tall and elegant, with a wide-brimmed hat, a summer frock and stylish white shoes. Her figure made me goggle as I showed her round the printing works. Sandy McMurchy, conservative in every sense, was struck dumb. Arthur Henderson had even less to say than usual. But when she visited Archie MacMillan in his hot corner, interrupting the clash and clatter of the linotype, he was more forthcoming.

'Happy in your work, Mr MacMillan?'

'As happy as I'll ever be.'

'You don't find the working conditions too uncomfortable? Too hot, for instance?'

'Ach, I've kent worse.'

I saw that his mind wasn't strictly on business. He smiled, jaws working, and looked the inspector up and down, the gleam in his eye that of a connoisseur. I realised that as far as his cynical temperament would allow he was becoming excited.

She gave him back his smile. 'I notice you chew tobacco, Mr MacMillan. Do *all* printers chew tobacco?'

'Ay, maist o' them. They canna smoke, ye see, workin' wi' baith hands.'

'I think it's a most unfortunate habit. Look at the condition of the floor all round you!'

Archie stared at her. His goddess was letting him down. Besides, as a result of increasing excitement, a large tobacco spittle was forming in his mouth. 'Nicotine doesna rot the wood,' he mumbled. 'It's a kind o' disinfectant. A kind o' preservative.'

She laughed. 'That's a new one on me!'

The laugh did it. Involuntarily, and without taking his usual careful aim, Archie spat. A stream of brown saliva landed on the toe of a white shoe.

I leapt for a rag and wiped the shoe clean, enjoying, as a bonus, a close-up view of slender, silk-clad ankles.

Fortunately, this particular inspector had a sense of humour. She and Archie parted friends. In her report the works were rated 'satisfactory'.

At that time Campbeltown supported another printing establishment, a relic of the defunct *Argyllshire Herald*. The gaffer there was the late Bob Albin.

Most printers, under a camouflage of irritable superiority towards writers and editors, are entertaining company. For this reason I became friendly not only with the *Courier* staff but also with Bob.

He was a Glasgow man, only a few years older than myself, with a gentle wit and the same naive concern for justice as I had. One night, in my digs, he told me a remarkable story of his grandfather: a story of Victorian Glasgow which had such far-reaching social effects that I am at a loss to understand why it remains comparatively unknown. The documents in the case were all in Bob's possession. Most of them are now in mine. They form the basis of the narrative which follows.

Thomas Albin was a prosperous hairdresser. In the late nineteenth century his main barber's shop was in Milton Street, in the Cowcaddens; but he owned five branches in other parts of Glasgow. Forty-three years old, he was happily married, with a young family. His only anxiety, not a serious one, was the health of his eldest son, Tom, who had just been made a partner in the business on his twenty-first birthday. But then, one cold spring night, something happened which changed not only his placid way of life but also the law of Scotland.

A typical Victorian, yet fussy and obstinate, Thomas Albin was a devoted churchman with whom family honour counted for everything. His children found him a hard disciplinarian, yet they were all, on the word of his grandson, extremely fond of him.

Despite an old-fashioned background he had many ideas in advance of his time. Some of the first public baths in Glasgow were installed at his Plantation Street shop. He also invented and manufactured a hair-restorer, well-known and popular in Glasgow, called Hirstuterine. According to the advertisement it was a cure for 'narcosis folliculorum, which is a degeneration of the follicles, with consequent atrophy of the hair'.

On the night of 10 March, 1893, he and young Tom stayed late in the Milton Street shop, putting up some electric light fittings. Glasgow Town Council had just begun to use electricity instead of gas, and Thomas Albin & Son was one of the few private firms to follow their lead at once.

They left the shop just before eleven o'clock. Thomas Albin went straight to his house at 439 Garscube Road, but young Tom said he needed fresh air and would take a walk. An hour later, Thomas Albin and his wife were still waiting for their son to come home.

Soon after midnight a police constable knocked at the door in Garscube Road. He brought a message. Young Tom had been taken to Camperdown Police Station. His father was wanted there.

Thomas Albin arrived at the Station to be told that his son was was in a cell, unconscious.

Inspector McKay said: 'He was found by two constables in Cedar Street, about an hour ago, lying against the railings of a church. When they brought him in, a charge was entered against him.'

'A charge! What charge?'

'Drunk and incapable, Mr Albin.'

'That's impossible. Not Tom. He left me outside the shop at eleven o'clock, perfectly well and sober. Inspector, you must get a doctor.'

'Dr Bruce, the divisional surgeon, has already seen him. There was nothing he could do. He telephoned for an ambulance, which ought to be here in a minute or two.'

'Didn't he question the charge? Tom has never been the worse for drink.'

'Dr Bruce was informed of the charge. He made no objection.'

'But my son is a teetotaller. It must be his heart. We were warned about his heart. . . .'

They went to the cell. Young Tom was lying on the floor. His face and hands were streaked with dirt. The legs of his trousers were frayed, the toe-caps of his boots worn into holes.

Startled by the appearance of his son, Thomas Albin went on his knees beside him. He tried the pulse, put a hand beneath the torn shirt and felt for a heart-beat. There was none. Young Tom was dead.

Inspector McKay was shocked. He was even more shocked when Thomas Albin, recovering, began to speak with rising hysteria.

'You killed him! The police killed him! I see it now. He had a heart attack. The constables jumped to the conclusion that he was drunk. They dragged him here. Look at his trousers, look at the toe-caps of his boots. They dragged him here face downwards like a brute beast!'

'But the doctor. . . .'

'Dr Bruce took your word for it. He could have saved him.'

'You are making a serious allegation, Mr Albin.'

'How long was Dr Bruce here?'

'I'm not sure. A few minutes.'

'A few minutes! How could he make a thorough examination in a few minutes? And my son dying! Inspector, I will see the chief constable. In spite of the charge my son died sober. Whatever happens I must clear his name.'

After the funeral was over Thomas Albin saw Chief Constable Boyd, who agreed to hold a private inquiry. When the two constables, the station inspector and Dr Bruce had all been interviewed and questioned, the chief constable delivered his verdict.

'I have gone into the matter thoroughly, Mr Albin. You have

my deepest sympathy, of course, but on examination of the
evidence I must disagree with your views on the case. I find that
the constables acted with the utmost humanity towards your son
and that Dr Bruce came to the only possible conclusion regarding
his death. As far as I am concerned the matter is now closed.'

The charge of drunk and incapable against young Tom remained
in the charge-book.

His father's next step was to write to the Town Clerk.

Dear Sir,

I am aware that fatal accidents in Scotland are not the subject of
public inquiry as in England, but in this case can something not be
done to clear the memory of my dear boy from an intolerable
stigma? In spite of Dr Bruce's opinion, I am convinced he was the
victim of a seizure, aggravated not by drink but by the rough and
inhumane treatment of the police. He was never under the influence
of drink in his life and was more inclined to avoid company than
to court it. It is a most serious tragedy, and I beg of you to do
something to have his name removed from the charge-book at
Camperdown Police Station.

Yours faithfully,
Thomas Albin.

The letter was considered by the council, but on the grounds
that no reason existed to doubt the police and medical evidence,
it was allowed to lie on the table. The only dissentient voice was
that of Councillor Wallace, a notorious radical.

'My Lord Provost,' he said, 'I am surprised by the moderation
of Mr Albin's letter. The man's right. There has been gross negli-
gence. Something should be done at once to protect the public
against such blunders—blunders by the police, blunders by the
doctors. It has happened before.'

At this point, according to a report in the *Glasgow Evening News*,
there was uproar. When it subsided, the Lord Provost remarked
smoothly that while he appreciated the point made by his esteemed
colleague, he was sure no good purpose could be served by taking
further action.

Whereupon Councillor Wallace became even more incensed.
'It's always the same!' he shouted. 'Officialdom must be upheld at

the expense of the human spirit. But I tell you, the human spirit will prevail in the end!'

He sat down. Unmoved by rhetoric, the councillors went on to deal with the next item on the agenda.

When informed of the council's decision, Thomas Albin grew bitter and withdrawn. He seldom went to the Milton Street Branch or attended to the business of his other shops. Trade was declining. The family was suffering from his alternate bouts of anger and depression. He looked pale and ill.

Then a new idea revived his spirit. The chief constable had let him down. So had the town council. What about the newspapers? With the help of a young reporter, who sometimes went for a hair-cut to the Milton Street shop, he arranged a meeting with the editor of the *Glasgow Evening News* and told him the story.

At first the editor was sceptical. In the end, however, Thomas Albin's grim honesty was able to win him over. It occurred to him, too, as a journalist, that here was the germ of a sensational news feature, which might reinforce the growing demand for a Fatal Accidents Enquiry Act for Scotland.

Next day, 10 April, 1893, the *Glasgow Evening News* came out with headlines:

CORONERS' INQUESTS IN SCOTLAND

Do we want them?

The Case for the Affirmative

In England, when a case of sudden death is reported, a public inquiry is always held. It is otherwise in Scotland. The system of private inquiry is open to serious objections when charges of maltreatment are made against the police, as in the case of young Albin.

The official account is that he died 'drunk and incapable'. Against this we give his father's statement. 'Not only did the police maltreat my son. The doctor took it for granted that he was under the influence of drink and made no effort to sustain life, but walked callously off, leaving him to die in a police cell on a false charge. There wasn't even a drop of water with which to moisten the dying boy's lips.'

Our readers will agree that in the circumstances Mr Albin is fully entitled to a public hearing. The evidence is conflicting and could only be properly sifted in open court. That it cannot be so sifted is a blot on our legal system which should be removed at once.

This article created a stir, not only in Glasgow but throughout Scotland. Letters began to appear in the *Evening News*.

The Albin case has proved how much we need Coroners' Inquests in Scotland. The truth is being concealed under an official conspiracy of silence. (*One Interested*. Glasgow, 11 April, 1893.)

Are the constables who conveyed young Albin to the police office, the inspector who booked the charge, and the divisional surgeon who did not examine him, to retain their situations without censure? (*Pro Bono Publico*. 11 April, 1893.)

In face of Mr Albin's statement, surely it is time that policemen, inspectors, divisional surgeons and even chief constables were aware of the seemingly unknown fact that they are the servants of the people and that when gross mismanagement occurs, the public have a right to know the reason why. (*Searchlight*. Falkirk, 12 April, 1893.)

The *Glasgow Evening News* also printed statements by a number of Scottish MPs. These included one by Dr Cameron (later Sir Charles Cameron, Bt.), member for the College Division of Glasgow: 'The system of private inquiry in cases of sudden death is unfair and dangerous. I should welcome a Fatal Accidents Enquiry Act for Scotland.'

Thomas Albin was bewildered by the turn events had taken. The public were now indignant on his behalf, but in their demand for new legislation they were forgetting about young Tom. The Albin case was the talk of the country and might lead to an Act of Parliament, but his son's name remained in the charge-book. The newspapers were publishing long articles about a Fatal Accidents Enquiry Act, but he wanted them to publish the truth— that Dr Bruce and the police were mistaken and that young Tom had died without a stain on his character.

His business was going down: he didn't care. He felt ill: that

Southend village with golf course and Sanda Island

Southend parish kirk

Top: Sailor Jeck

Bottom: Sailor Jeck, with
fishermen friends, 1912

Top: 'Shooting his line'. Captain Willie MacVicar, MBE

Bottom: How to follow through!

Jean, in contemplative mood

Presenter, *Songs of Praise*, Elgin St Giles'

didn't worry him. He stayed at home, gaunt, ill-tempered uninterested in anything except the memory of his son.

He had another talk with the young reporter. Patiently the latter
pointed out that before the newspapers could publish the truth as
Mr Albin saw it the charge-book at Camperdown Police Station
would have to be altered, under instructions from either the Lord
Advocate or the Crown Agent in Edinburgh.

'But why don't you write to your MP, Dr Cameron, who seems
to be in favour of public inquiries, and ask him to raise the matter
in Parliament? The Lord Advocate may then take notice. There's
one significant thing,' added the reporter. 'After all that has been
said in the press, neither Dr Bruce nor the police have made any
attempt to defend themselves. They know they were wrong: I'm
convinced of it.'

With new hope, Thomas Albin wrote to Dr Cameron on 13
April. On 21 April the member for the College Division of Glasgow
asked a question in the House of Commons. It charged the police
with carelessness, but—and this is what disappointed the dour
seeker after justice—it made no reference to Dr Bruce's part in the
case. The Lord Advocate's reply upheld the police evidence and
did nothing at all to clear young Tom.

On the same day, in answer to a question from Mr John Leng,
member for Dundee, the Lord Advocate said that he intended
shortly to introduce a Fatal Accidents Enquiry Bill for Scotland.

But this important statement was no comfort to Thomas Albin.
He had failed again. Dr Cameron's question had been a political
one, a mere prop for the new Act. Young Tom's name was still in
the charge-book.

His wife, his family and his friends all tried to persuade him to
give up the uneven struggle. He was ruining his health and his
business, they told him. His behaviour was antagonising the police
and the medical profession. Even the press, which had done so
much for him, was beginning to look askance at his outspoken
comments. In any case, they said, everybody who counted now
believed that young Tom was innocent.

But Thomas Albin was obdurate. The charge against his son
still stood. It must be struck out or altered. The authorities must
be made to admit their mistake.

Then, from a reading of back numbers of the newspapers, he discovered something which appeared to him highly important. He made an appointment to see Dr Cameron when the MP was in Glasgow about the end of April.

At first the interview went well enough. Dr Cameron expressed personal sympathy but said that in law the process of striking out a charge was difficult and complicated.

'To me, sir.' said Thomas Albin, 'it is very simple. As I told you before in my letter, everything depends on Dr Bruce's evidence, which was mistaken. If he'd made a thorough examination he would have found that my son was sober.'

'No doubt, Mr Albin. But Dr Bruce is a busy man.'

'Could *you* not persuade the Lord Advocate to delete the charge? You are a man of standing, of high position.'

'My dear sir, be reasonable. The Lord Advocate has more important business. Besides, the medical evidence is a matter for the local authorities.'

'But the local authorities are the police. And Dr Bruce. They won't admit their mistake.'

'Then what can *I* do? I am endeavouring to hasten the new Act.'

'You could endeavour to influence Dr Bruce, sir. He is a friend of yours. He has often been your chairman at political meetings.'

'True. But if he sincerely believes—'

'That my son was drunk? Is that what you mean?'

'Well . . .'

'I deny it! You are protecting Dr Bruce!' Suddenly Thomas Albin lost control. Resentment kept secret until now came tumbling out. 'Yes! On the night of my son's death, Dr Bruce could spend the whole evening on your platform, as your chairman. I read about it, Dr Cameron, just the other day. But he could not spend five minutes to save my boy's life or reputation!'

The interview ended in recrimination. Thomas Albin had lost another battle and another ally.

That evening, at home, he sat down and wrote to the Lord Advocate. It seemed to him the only course now open.

The letter was long and flowery, in the manner of the time, but the relevant paragraphs are these:

I would respectfully submit that your answer to the Honourable Member for the College Division was neither satisfactory nor conclusive. You say that my son fell on the street and was found in a position which would account for the state of his boots. Sir, I scarcely think that a mere fall would knock holes in the toes of his boots . . .

It is with the utmost reluctance and pain that I approach your Lordship. But the young man was my first-born, and from the day of his birth to his melancholy death had been my constant companion . . .

I beg of you to direct that the medical evidence be turned aside and that the charge against my son at the Camperdown Police Station be removed from the charge-book.

A few days later Thomas Albin received a reply from the Lord Advocate's secretary. After a reference to the 'painful' circumstances of the case, the letter went on:

His Lordship desires me to add that he does not see that further proceedings could be usefully directed by him in the matter.

Suffering from exhaustion and strain, Thomas Albin was put to bed by his doctor, but again and again, with brave persistence, he wrote to the Lord Advocate. The answer to his fifth letter was chilling.

I beg to acknowledge your letter of 15 May and am directed by his Lordship to state definitely and finally that there is nothing to add to what has been stated in previous communications.

That afternoon, as he lay in bed, Thomas Albin was visited by the young reporter who had been his friend and confidant almost from the start.

'I'm sorry, Mr Albin. This letter appears to be conclusive. Whitehall isn't going to help.'

'They are so hard, impersonal, so dazzled by affairs of state that they forget the ordinary people who make up the state. But I am not discouraged. I have been thinking: should I get in touch with Robert Blatchford?'

'You mean the editor of the *Clarion*?'

'Yes. He is a supporter of lost causes. He might understand.'

'You have an idea there, Mr Albin. The *Clarion* has more influence with the rank and file than any other paper in the kingdom.'

'I am not well. Could you help me to put my case?'

'Of course. I will write to Blatchford now, in your name.'

Thomas Albin had a quick reply from the *Clarion* Office in Corporation Street, Manchester:

Dear Sir,
    'Will you please send on the papers in the case? We will see what can be done.
                                        Yours sincerely,
                                            R. Blatchford.

What could be done was done immediately. The *Clarion* came out with a sensational article on its leader page. It went into every detail of the case and thundered out into a final paragraph:

In view of the facts recorded above, in view of the guilty silence of doctor and police, it is clear that young Tom Albin was innocent. In the name of the people we demand that his name be cleared of the foul stigma imposed upon it. In the name of the people we echo the cry of a devoted father, 'Justice for my son !'

The article itself might have left Whitehall cold. Its repercussions were what counted. On the first day after publication some 200 letters demanding action were delivered to the Lord Advocate's office. MPs opening their mail found that every second letter referred to the Albin case. A sackful of correspondence supporting Thomas Albin was forwarded to the Prime Minister by Robert Blatchford.

The Lord Advocate found himself in a jam and decided, following a time honoured principle, that he must wriggle out of it as best he could. This he did by referring the matter to the Crown Agent in Edinburgh, with a recommendation that something should be done—and quickly. Such as deleting the charge against young Tom Albin. Such as censuring the police.

A day or two later Thomas Albin was still in bed, gradually recovering from his illness. His wife, Agnes, was in the room, talking to him. It was a hot, stuffy morning in early summer and the sound of traffic in Garscube road could be heard through the open window.

The young reporter came in. 'Great news, Mr Albin, and you are directly responsible for it! The Fatal Accidents Enquiry Bill has been issued in Parliament.'

'My boy, I am glad. But Agnes and I have better news for you than that. A letter came today, from the Crown Office in Edinburgh.'

'About your son?'

'Yes. It's on the table there. Agnes, let him see it.' Then, as the reporter opened the blue envelope, he added: 'Read it aloud to us.'

> *Crown Office, Edinburgh.*
> 27 *May*, 1893.
> *To Thomas Albin.*
> Dear Sir,
>   On instructions from the Lord Advocate, I have been in communication with the Glasgow Police Authorities in regard to your son's death. I am now to inform you that a note has been added to the entry in the charge-book at Camperdown, in the following terms: 'It was supposed that Albin was drunk and incapable, but this has been found not to be the case. It is established he was suffering from heart disease, of which he died in the Police Office.'
>   I am, Your obedient servant,
>   John Cowan, Crown Agent.

Seeking justice, Thomas Albin almost ruined his health and his business. He lost friends and put at risk family loyalty and affection. But in the end he found what he sought and cleared the name of his dead son.

For the victory he owed thanks to democracy. Democracy owed thanks—and always will owe thanks—to a free and independent press.

As a postscript to the case, there are two questions which occur to me. Why, at the beginning, was the Albin family doctor not called in to rebut Dr Bruce's hasty diagnosis? And why, in all the documents and newspaper cuttings so carefully preserved by

Thomas Albin, is there not a single word of comment, protest or apology from Dr Bruce?

During my time on the *Courier* the idea of holding a regatta in Campbeltown Loch was considered by the town council.

Before World War I, regattas had been regular and popular features of a 'Wee Toon' summer and several councillors believed they could be revived with success. I agreed with their opinion, because Campbeltown's landlocked harbour, sheltered on one side by Bengullion and on the other by Cnoc Scalbert, offers a beautiful setting for white sails and flashing oars.

At the time nothing came of the suggestion, but from Alec MacLeod and the printers I learned a great deal about the happiness and fun derived from old-time regattas.

One story about Campbeltown's last regatta particularly appealed to me, because its central character was a lady called Sailor Jeck. I had heard about Sailor Jeck before, from the fishermen at the Old Quay Head; but now, as I listened to the tale of her participation in the Ladies' Race, she began to come alive for me. I recognised her as a living woman and came to understand how tragic and unjust had been the circumstances of her death.

Alec MacLeod well remembered the excitement in the town before this regatta. On the tar-scented pier, where gulls cackled above the herring boats, where puffers took on coal amid the clanking of steam winches and the ribald jokes of the 'lumpers', bets were laid on the outcome of the races. Sailor Jeck, whose real name was Agnes Morrison, made as much noise as the men and backed her favourites with equal enthusiasm.

She was an unusual character. A powerful woman of middle height, with glossy brown hair hanging to her shoulders, she could lift a hundredweight sack of coal as if it were a baby. She worked as a quay 'lumper', on an equal footing with the men, and her language had an edge that even her male colleagues found hard to match.

She owned a small boat, a kind of harbour taxi. On one occasion it was hired by a Frenchman, whom she rowed ashore from his ship in the harbour. Deceived by her good nature and by the

feminine fripperies on her shawl and petticoat, he tried to escape
without paying his due. But she pursued him along the pier,
caught him by the hair of his head and neatly pitched him back
into the boat—all this without once removing from her mouth
a favourite short clay pipe. The Frenchman paid.

The most popular betting medium at the regatta was the Ladies'
Race. This was because the competitors, as a rule, came from
the ranks of local society, and their skill with the oars was so
erratic that the winner often proved to be someone entirely
unexpected.

At this last regatta the ante-post favourite was a schoolmaster's
daughter called Jenny, who had been seen practising with a
certain amount of *élan*. It was rumoured that in a trial outing she
had completed the quarter-mile course in twenty-five minutes—
after losing her oars only once—and though this was far from being
a record, the fact remained that the form of some of the other
ladies made it seem unlikely they would finish at all.

With her long fair hair and spannable waist and her prim little
smile contrasting with the mischief in her eyes, Jenny was inclined
to be a snob.

'A wee scunner, that's what she is!' growled a young fisherman
named Eddie, whose father owned half-a-dozen skiffs. 'I asked her
for a dance last night and she wouldna ha'e me,' he explained to
his mates. 'Off she went wi' a flannelled exciseman. Peter Thomson,
ye ken. By gosh, I'm goin' tae teach her a lesson!'

'Good for yoursel', Eddie!' they encouraged him 'What ha'e
ye in mind?'

'Wait and see,' he said.

The day of the regatta was warm and sunny, with scarcely a
capful of wind, an almost incredible state of affairs on the second
Saturday of the Glasgow Fair. The sailing dinghies drifted off
Davaar Island at the mouth of the Loch, white butterflies hovering
motionless; but no one paid them much attention, for it would
be hours before they crossed the finishing line. The main interest
of the spectators, gathered in cheerful masses on both quays
and in small boats in the harbour itself, was centred on the
rowing.

At three o'clock the ladies were called to the starting line. According to Alec MacLeod, Jenny was ravishing in a large picture hat and billowing skirt so short that her ankles were like magnets to men's eyes.

Her rivals manoeuvred alongside her. One was the plump daughter of a banker, who giggled and handled her oars as if they were red-hot pokers. Another was the horsey-looking wife of a distiller. She had become popular with the fishermen because she could swear at them if the need arose but never forgot their wives and children when catches were poor.

And suddenly, around the end of the New Quay, there appeared a fourth competitor. She wore a hat like Jenny's, which concealed her face, and a blouse as red as the marking buoys. But what intrigued the spectators most of all was the expert way she handled her boat. As it approached the line a white wave creamed under the bow.   Peter Thomson, white-flannelled and acting as an official in the judge's whaler, yelled out: 'It's Sailor Jeck! *She* can't compete!'

'Why no'?' yelled back Eddie, belligerently waving his fist from the bow of his father's skiff, the *Stella Spei*. 'She's a wumman: ye canna deny it!'

'It's not fair? She's as strong as a man!'

At which Eddie's blue-guernseyed allies put their fingers to their noses and shouted across the water: 'She's a wumman a' the same!'

In the midst of the commotion the starter fired his pistol. Sailor Jeck's boat leaped ahead, like a frigate from a line of puffers, and in a matter of seconds was twenty yards in front of Jenny's. The other two ladies, so the story goes, didn't start at all. Laughter and catcalls drowned the bellows of annoyance from the betting men.

True to her bargain, Sailor Jeck finished the course. Then, shipping her oars, she took time to survey the scene. Jenny had lost her hat and was leaning across the gun'le of her boat sobbing with mortification. The judge's whaler and the *Stella Spei* had drifted together and Eddie and Peter Thomson were scrapping like schoolboys on the deck of the skiff.

Sailor Jeck had been well paid by Eddie. Now, eyeing Jenny,

she understood for the first time what lay behind the so-called 'joke'.

Blue eyes became frosty; powerful arms sent her boat surging back to the *Stella Spei*. A few moments later delighted spectators saw her climb nimbly aboard and catch Eddie and Peter by the scruffs of their necks. As she brought their heads together the crack could be heard all over the harbour. And as she flung them overboard the splashes narrowly preceded a happy roar of approval and applause.

Triumphantly, arms akimbo, Sailor Jeck stood alone in the bow of the *Stella Spei*, while policemen came thundering down the pier, prepared to quell a riot.

Jenny looked up at her. Their eyes met and a strange thing happened. A little shyly, the two women smiled to each other.

Here existed gaiety and the summer sun. Sailor Jeck was a heroine, a 'character' admired by all. Stories about her gained colourful detail at every telling. But she was independent, perhaps a little too proud, and there was no Welfare State to care for her.

Soon after the last regatta she became ill. I think her trouble must have been a chest complaint, though neither Alec MacLeod nor the *Courier* printers were certain about this. Her strength left her. She no longer worked on the pier with the other 'lumpers' but scraped a frugal existence by gathering whelks in season and, in summer, helping to lift early potatoes on the shore farms.

Shortly before World War I, along with half-a-dozen other 'tattie howkers', she was employed on a farm in Southend. It was, in fact, the Rat Stane farm. In those days the howkers were 'fee'd' by a contractor, who, in turn, was hired by the farmer and paid a lump sum to clear his fields. If the contractor was mean and profit-hungry, the money he gave his employees was shockingly meagre. As a rule the howkers slept at night in the farmer's barn, empty except for a few battles of straw to serve as beds, and I have been told that some of them, coarse-mouthed, lustful, hard-drinking and violent, turned their sleeping-quarters into Hogarthian hell's kitchens.

Sailor Jeck trudged and stooped along the drills, picking the potatoes out of the hard earth, filling her riddle and then emptying it into a sack. She was sick and exhausted, but nobody cared. The contractor told her to get a move on: he couldn't imagine that a 'gallus' character like Sailor Jeck might be in need of help. In the barn she slept among the straw apart from her companions. She was unmolested, because the legend of her strength of body and spirit lived on.

It was cold, wet weather for June, One night Sailor Jeck lay down in her damp clothes with a fever. In the morning she failed to get up, but the other 'howkers', uninterested, let her lie. Maybe she had a cold. If so, she was hardy and would soon recover.

In the evening, coming back from the fields, they found her dead.

It is unlikely that a similar tragedy could occur in today's more compassionate society. But in a spiritual context it happens often, even yet. Should any human being be cast aside, redundant? Is redundancy ever compatible with justice?

My most gruelling news beat on the *Courier* was when a violent explosion occurred in the submarine L26, then recharging batteries in Campbeltown harbour. In *Salt in My Porridge* I told how the injured were brought ashore by local skiffs and other small boats: 'Some of the injured men's features were unrecognisable. As first-aid was being rendered to one of them, I heard him mutter, "No good working with me. I'm through." But he lived.'

I saw him that ghastly afternoon for about ten seconds only, but his unselfish words remained in my mind. I didn't know his name or rank, but I knew that he had lived, because none of the casualties brought ashore in life had subsequently died.

He lived. He still does. Soon after the publication of *Salt in My Porridge* I had a letter from him. His name is Harry Taylor.

I had another letter, written independently, from his sister-in-law, Mrs Elizabeth Swan of Aytoun Road in Glasgow. After referring to my account of the explosion in the L26, she went on:

> The man you mention in your book who wanted others to be attended to before him was my brother-in-law, Harry Taylor. He was one of four seriously injured who were flown to the Western

Infirmary (in Glasgow). My own brother had broken his leg in a motor-bike accident the previous Sunday, and the four sailor lads were brought into his ward. As they had nobody to visit them regularly, my brother, my sister and I more or less adopted them.

Harry was the last to leave for the south. His ankle was shattered and they didn't amputate, knowing this might end his naval career. He had a ghastly time after reaching the Naval Hospital in Portsmouth, but my sister, May, kept writing to him.

To cut a long story short, Harry and May were married in Gosport in April, 1937. They now have a great big son, Archie, and two beautiful grandchildren. They are recently retired, living in a beautiful wee village called Ashover in Derbyshire.

Isn't that a nice *People's Friend* story in real life?

It certainly is. But life has a habit of dealing the cards of justice in an illogical way few fiction writers would have the nerve to copy.

Thomas Albin, Sailor Jeck, Harry Taylor. Does a pattern of justice emerge from their stories? I don't know. The problem has worried me all my life. Has justice anything to do with divinity? Or is it simply a product of blind chance, individual character and the whim of contemporary society?

7

Soldier of Fortune

When I gave up my job on the *Courier* to become a full-time freelance writer, Jean and I had to make a decision. Where, on getting married, should we establish a base of operations? Ought we to live in Glasgow, Edinburgh or London, in daily contact with publishers, editors, and producers at the BBC? Or ought we to stay in Southend, where we could have plenty of fresh air, a time-table of our own and a guarantee of friendly neighbours?

We decided to stay in Southend.

As far as my job was concerned the disadvantages were obvious. I should probably miss some of the 'instant' money available to an urban journalist. Knowledge of the world might be gained less easily in the countryside than in bustling streets. Dealing with publishers and editors by post could cause frustration.

We were, however, aware of advantages. In Southend I could view the world with more detachment than is possible in a city and this might have a beneficial effect on what I wrote. Since writing is a hard trade, dependent on physical fitness to sustain long, hunched hours at a typewriter, a life in the country would give me a better chance to cultivate health. (Though twenty cigarettes a day might cancel out some of the benefits.)

In any case, both Jean and I wanted to remain members of the community in which we had grown up. We reckoned that in return for some willing service it would give us comfort and the quality of life we wanted. The idea of becoming lone battlers in some asphalt jungle, though exciting, had no great appeal. Perhaps we were cowards. Who knows?

During the past forty years, however, we have never once regretted our decision. We have lost some battles and won others, but in dejection or in triumph we have always been conscious of a communal sympathy and discipline which maintained a balance. In a community where our lives, whether we like it or not, are open to inspection by our neighbours, where 'the giftie' affords us every opportunity of 'seeing oorsels as ithers see us', we can enjoy the luxury of acting naturally, without the necessity of acquiring alien airs and graces.

It may be argued that contentment of this kind tends to encourage a smug and vegetable existence. With us there was no danger of that. I had to fight hard in a savagely competitive market to sell the things I wrote. Jean, at times, had to keep house on a shoestring and a prayer. In addition, we took a full part in parish life and there was always something to struggle and campaign for as members of the kirk, as participants in amateur drama, as supporters of the life-boat, the Red Cross and other voluntary bodies. We argued doucely and made enemies. We spoke out in angry protest and made friends.

But all the time, in common with our neighbours, we felt that we counted, that we had some influence, however small, on life and affairs. I think we should have found it more difficult to feel this had we lived in an anonymous city. Indeed, I am sure that many of the current discontents spring from a suspicion that in a brassy new world of urban statistics the individual voice counts for nothing at all.

We were in no danger, either, of becoming too complacent, stuck in a parochial vacuum. World War II saw to that. Into six years I—and a million colleagues—packed a lifetime of adventure and travel; and Jean shared grief and anxiety with a million other young women of her day.

But the war came to an end, as all other evils do, and we can look back on it now, detached from its tragedies, as a time when the imminence of death brought us close to the meaning of life.

I find that the memories of war which readily occur to me today have nothing to do with death and destruction. If I make an effort, however, I can recall incidents that were hard to bear.

In Madagascar I knelt beside a boy dying of malaria and heard him calling for his mother.

Along a bare and dusty Sicilian road I went on a motor-bike to meet my brother Archie, with the Argylls, and found, at my journey's end, that he had died of wounds the previous day.

On a hilltop in Italy I stood among the snow, looking down at the dead face of a young officer, the last of five sons of a Dorset clergyman to have been killed in action.

In charge of a ration party near Lentini, I found a sergeant drunk, had him arrested, tried, reduced to the ranks and sent to an outlying company position, where in the first hour, he was killed.

One night at Anzio a jeep in front of mine was blown to pieces and I helped to gather into sacks the torn flesh of its occupants.

Another time at Anzio a hardened corporal tried to salute me and failed, because from head to toe he was shaking with what they now called battle fatigue but had been better described in World War I as shell shock.

On a cold, grey morning I drove a jeep past the Colosseum in Rome to a place smelling of blood and disinfectant and saw the body of my Sergeant Hunter, shot dead by drunken Americans.

And finally, when the war ended, a respected comrade came to me and wept, because on the day before his demob and a return, after years of honourable service, to his wife and family, he had contracted venereal disease.

A mental safety device locks such memories away, and the doors are opened only with difficulty. This may be one reason why wars recur. If everybody knew and remembered their effect on individual lives, surely they would be controlled to the point of eradication, like smallpox and bubonic plague. But the statistics of power and privilege oppose such an outcome, and those who live by statistics often seem willing to let others die by statistics.

I hate the idea of war and recognise the con-trick that made me a temporary soldier. By an effort of will I can recall human trage-dies that angered and daunted me. At the same time, if I am honest, I have to admit that certain aspects of my service were enjoyable and come easily to the surface of memory, like happy old photos in a drawer.

The odd thing about my career in the army is that in many ways, despite entanglements of red tape, I was able to control its course.

After spending several months at Stirling Castle and in Tillicoultry, learning to be a soldier and being taught how to drive bren-gun carriers up and across impossible ridges, I was sent to Droitwich for the purpose of becoming an officer specialising in machine-guns. How or why I was chosen to suffer such a fate I cannot imagine. Did a clerk in some obscure office put a tick after the wrong name?

Anyway, I wanted nothing to do with Droitwich or machine-guns. I wanted to be an officer in a Scots infantry regiment, where the staple drink would be whisky and not uninspiring mild and bitter. So I went to the commanding officer of the Training Unit and told him, politely, that I had changed my mind about becoming an officer. Such glories were not for a humble scribe, I said. He argued with me like a father, but I stuck to my guns (or, rather, insisted that I didn't stick to them) and within a week was back at Stirling Castle. There, parading Scottish Nationalism, I explained my position to a sympathetic Selection Board. In a remarkably short time I found myself at Dunbar, with an Officer Cadet Training Unit (Infantry).

This was more like it. Unfortunately, the drill sergeant-major turned out to be a mean-spirited tyrant, and my fellow cadets and I spent a great deal of time concocting plans to humiliate him when we got pips on our shoulders. (I never did see him again.) For the first month we drilled and exercised like Spartans. Luckily, I had been an athlete, and for me the regime was not so much a burden as for some others.

The climax to this period came with a visit to the open-air swimming pool, where all of us, whether we could swim of not, were required to jump thirty feet off the high diving-board. PT corporals swam in the water below to rescue the perishing. With careless self-confidence I essayed a dive instead of a nose-holding jump and did a belly-flop. For days afterwards I suffered from stomach ache and bruising, but I kept the pain to myself.

Then we began three months of tactical training. We were formed into an imaginary battalion with different cadets acting each week as commanding officer, platoon commanders, platoon sergeants and section corporals. I looked at the notice-board detailing the appointments for the first week and saw, to my horror, that I had been named as cadet CO.

The following morning I had to march the 'battalion' from a rendezvous outside the Bellevue Hotel down through the town to the barracks. I felt like an idiot out there on my own, with hundreds of boots thudding inexorably behind me and girls and small boys uttering wolf-whistles as I passed. Then, along the street in front, I saw an officer approaching on a bicycle.

What in heaven's name did a 'battalion commander' do on meeting an officer on a bicycle? In vain I tried to recall a military regulation covering such a crisis. An impression glimmered in my brain that officers on bicycles ought to be ignored, for the simple reason that they might find it difficult to return a salute. However, I decided to take no chances and, if I was going to make a mistake, to make it in a spectacular fashion.

As the officer came within ten yards of me I bellowed at the pitch of my voice: 'Battalion! Eyes left.' For my part, while marching on, I brought up my right arm in a quivering salute.

The effect on the officer, a young and popular member of the OCTU staff, was startling. He fell off his bicycle.

I lowered my arm and yelled, 'Eyes front!' But not before I'd caught a glimpse of the unfortunate officer scrambling up and standing stiffly at the salute, with the bicycle wreckage tangled about his feet.

I expected repercussions. None came, Nobody mentioned the incident again, and I still don't know whether I acted properly or not.

On the whole, I was happy at Dunbar.

In leisure hours we were permitted to play on the historic golf course, which, incidentally, was the camping site of Cromwell's army before the Battle of Dunbar in 1650. The fact that I lost about a dozen balls, slicing into the trees of the Deer Park at the first hole, is submerged in recollection of a 4 iron tee-shot placed inches from the pin at The Narrows, the 168 yard 16th.

Another good memory is of the late Sam Milliken and his wife, Jenny. Both contemporaries of mine at Campbeltown

Grammar School, by then married and settled in as respected citizens of the town, they kept open house for me and any of my friends I cared to bring along. Sam was a banker, medically unfit for active service. Jenny was a charmer, a vivacious foil for her husband's sardonic humour. Though childless, they acted *in loco parentis* for the benefit of slightly disorientated louts like 'the cadets'. Our gratitude was boundless for civilised food, drink and conversation.

Believing I had done reasonably well as a prospective officer, I looked forward to the passing out parade. But pride is always dangerous. On a night exercise somewhere in the Lammermuir Hills I sat on a piece of barbed wire, put a dressing on the wound myself and imagined that a couple of days would find it healed. Instead, it developed into a carbuncle. I was taken to hospital, given a spinal anaesthetic by means of the largest and most forbidding syringe I have ever seen, placed on an operating table with my legs slung high and allowed to watch a surgeon removing the carbuncle from a position dangerously near my testicles. The passing out parade was held while I recovered from the ordeal; but, to my pleasure and relief, I was given my pips, *in absentia*.

A few weeks later I was posted to the 2nd Battalion, the Royal Scots Fusiliers, as an officer with the Carrier Platoon of HQ Company.

For a time we trained at Enniskillen, in Northern Ireland, receiving the utmost hospitality from the farmers over whose land we exercised. This may have been because a majority were themselves of Scots descent.

One night, waiting in the lee of a barn for a 'dawn attack', my men and I were discovered by the farmer and his wife, up early for the milking. Would we, they asked, like some ham and eggs to keep out the cold? Would we like like some ham and eggs! The dawn attack came and went. It was ignored. Encouraged by the farmer, who remained happily in our company, the boys and I lay among the straw in the barn, digesting the ham and eggs and polishing off a bottle of Scotch I had thoughtfully provided as part of my haversack ration.

I liked the RSF. I began to make friends, among them Norman

Milne, Charlie Cope, Alan Pettigrew, Jack Bowie, Frank Jones and Adam MacFarlan, another minister's son. (They are all still my friends.) Then the blow fell. An edict was issued from the War Office that junior officers who were 'old'—i.e., over 30—should be transferred from the dangerous infantry to 'easier' outfits like Ordnance and the Pioneers. Being 33, I was in line for such a posting, and sure enough the CO sent for me one morning to intimate that my future lay with the Royal Army Service Corps. In India, of all places.

This was insufferable. I was a Royal Scots Fusilier. I wanted to remain one and spend the rest of the war with men I had learnt to understand and respect. What could I do to bend the War Office to my will?

First of all I tried writing to the MP for Argyll. He was polite but as helpful in the situation as my batman, Fusilier McClymont. Then I remembered 'my illness'. The doctor in the Glasgow nursing home had talked vaguely about an Eastern disease. Would he come to my aid by certifying that if I were sent to India my illness might recur. He would, and he did. Reading his letter, the CO said, 'Seems we can't get rid of you yet.' I remained with the RSF.

A few weeks later it became known that the 5th Division, of which the 2nd RSF formed a part, was being sent to India. From Enniskillen we travelled by train, ship and train again to Caterham, Surrey, where we began collecting tropical kit.

The CO sent for me. 'What happens now? That medical certificate . . . '

'I don't remember it, sir.'

'H'm. Neither do I.'

So, by way of Madagascar, I went with the battalion to India. I contracted malaria there, both malignant and benign. But that is another story.

From India we went to a place called Qum in Persia. There, among the snow, I was appointed Mechanical Transport Officer. The army moves in mysterious ways. Being Mechanical Transport Officer meant that though cam-shafts and carburettors were double-Dutch in my vocabulary I was in charge of about 150 skilled men, along with vehicles and equipment worth hundreds of thousands of pounds.

In the outcome, however, I had few worries. Sergeant Hunter (general discipline), Sergeant Hibbett (vehicle administration), Sergeant Telfer (REME), Corporal Dunwoody (stores) and Corporal Paterson (clerk) ran the section for me with awesome efficiency. Fusilier Jelen, a tailor in civvie street, cut my hair as stylishly as he had cut cloth. Fusilier Ought-six Kane, when he wasn't 'accidentally' killing geese and chickens with his truck or swiping goods like tea, sugar, razor-blades and cigarettes from unsuspecting pals at NAAFI stores, supplied me with stimulating floods of rich, stewed tea. When circumstances allowed, Fusilier McClymont ('Jaggy Feet') saw to it that I had a reasonably comfortable bed at night.

Towards the end of the war I was offered command of a company but persuaded the CO to allow me to remain with the MT section until my 'demob'. The men and I had become used to each other, and it seemed to me that the resultant relationships, built on mutual trust, ought to be maintained for as long as possible. To abandon them for the sake of promotion was, as far as I was concerned, an idea even less attractive than leaving Southend to live in a big city.

Luck stayed with me. Most of the MT Section said goodbye to the army at approximately the same time as I did.

Transporting the battalion and its equipment from Persia across Iraq to Syria and the Lebanon, from the Lebanon by sea to Sicily, from Sicily through Italy and thence by ship to Marseilles, from Marseilles along the valley of the Rhone to Belgium and from Belgium by way of Holland to Lübeck in Germany was an adventurous business requiring nerve and, above all, considerable mechanical skill. The men of the MT Section, ignoring the whims and fancies of their officer, especially in the areas of mechanical repairs and map-reading, carried through the assignment without experiencing any major crisis. On the way we encountered our quota of wine, women and song and enjoyed as rich a geographical education as Burton and Speke.

From the snows of the Paitak Pass we descended in convoy to the warmer plains. On the ancient royal highway leading from Ecbatana (Hamadan) to Babylon we stopped near the cross-roads at

Behistun to look up at a high cliff. There, 160 feet above us, we saw the famous inscription which includes the words: *I, Darius, King of Kings, King of the Whole World.*

A self-composed catalogue of the achievements of King Darius I of Persia, it is in three languages, Persian, Elamite and Babylonian. Though carved out of solid rock in 520 BC and ever since exposed to water trickling down over the edge of the cliff, it still remains legible. Omitted from the text is any reference to Marathon, where Darius's Persian army was defeated by the Greeks.

Sergeant Hunter, Ought-six Kane and I thought the whole thing a bit of a giggle. Darius had considered himself the most powerful and privileged being in the world and had employed a thousand slaves to fashion his memorial. But who the hell cared two hoots about his power and privilege today? The same fate, we told each other, would be bloody Hitler's. In 2500 years would anybody even remember the perverted little bastard? To us, insignificant specks on the vast, inhospitable desert that was our vision of Persia, the thought was comforting.

In days to come we were to visit the ruined 'temples' at Baalbek, with their haunting resemblance to a modern rocket launching-pad. We were to see, sunk beneath the clear warm waters of the Mediterranean, the quays and stone bollards of the ancient harbour of Tyre and to imagine, tied up against them, 'quinquiremes of Nineveh' exchanging their cargoes 'of ivory, and apes and peacocks' for ones of rich cloth dyed in the 'Tyrian purple'. We were to look up from the arid dust roads at the crumbling *kraks* of the Crusaders silhouetted against the Syrian sky, redundant sentinels keeping watch on nothing. We were to find, near the roadside, the source of the Orontes, a crystal pool continually replenished by water gushing from a cleft in the rock, and to emerge after a swim in its ice-cold depths feeling cleansed and purified like young gods. But it was the Behistun inscription which impressed us most of all. Power and privilege is the short-lived spawn of human vanity. 'What is a man profited, if he shall gain the whole world, and lose his own soul?' Or so, vain in our humility, we kept telling each other.

Each night, during our long trek, we parked out vehicles by the roadside, within a laager of barbed wire coils. Most of my drivers slept inside their trucks, in comfortable corners among the stores. An exception was Fusilier Darroch, in charge of the water truck. He and I used sleeping bags and lay in the open under the stars. He was from Jura. I was from Kintyre. To men of Argyll, descended from fighting clansmen who often slept rough and damp among the heather, the cool night air of the Middle East was no hardship. Neither Darroch nor I was punctilious about military usage or discipline. Highlanders seldom are. If we found ourselves bedded down within talking distance he would tell me about his home and family on Jura, and about Greta, the land-girl he hoped to marry when the war was over. I would tell him about Jean and Jock and Achnamara.

More than twenty years later, as chairman of the Uist and Bernera Gathering in the Highlanders Institute in Glasgow, I announced a Gaelic singer named on the programme as Iain Darroch. To my astonishment, black moustached and resplendent in Highland dress, Fusilier Darroch advanced from the wings, waving his wrist-lace in my direction. It was our first meeting since the war and we celebrated it there on the platform, to the surprise and amusement of the audience.

Not long ago Jean and I were guests at a dinner with the Glasgow Jura Association. Iain was the president, so we sat beside him and his wife, Greta. Life was good for all of us. The lonely and nostalgic nights in Persia made it seem even better for Iain and me.

One of those nights was spent a few miles outside the town of Kermanshah. I woke in the dawn, about six o'clock, with something nagging at my memory. Kermanshah? What did I know about Kermanshah? Then, recollecting a letter from Jean, I had it. Angus MacQueen, who had beaten me in the 100 yards at the School sports as often as I had beaten him, was a banker there, married and with a baby daughter. Could I find him and exchange greetings with him in the two hours remaining before the convoy was due to move on? At least I could try.

I shook Sergeant Hunter reluctantly awake and, ignoring groans and protests, told him where I was going. In the grey light I spurted off on my motor-bike.

Even at that early hour Kermanshah was busy with people. In a street in the lower part of the town I spotted a Persian gentleman who looked both alert and intelligent and asked him if he knew where Mr MacQueen, the banker, lived. He nodded and said, 'Sure,' in an American accent. Would he, for a consideration, guide me to Mr MacQueen's house? Sure he would: no trouble. Bundling up his Mohamet-ready tail-bag, he sat astride my pillion. Through the market-place and up the hill the Norton's motor gunned us to an area of expensive-looking houses. Suddenly my Persian friend tapped my shoulder and pointed towards one of them. I slowed down and stopped. 'There,' he said, importantly, 'resides Mr MacQueen.' We bade each other goodbye in a flurry of mutual esteem.

Around the wide verandah were a number of doors. From behind one of them came snoring sounds. I opened it and peered in. A large man with a military moustache and a partially bald head lay comfortably among tumbled sheets. He, assuredly, was not Angus.

I went to another door. It was also unlocked and I pushed it open, cautiously. This time I struck oil. In bed with his blonde wife was Angus, close-curled fair hair dishevelled. He had on a dress shirt and black tie.

I went in and prodded his shoulder. He came slowly to life, looked up at me with a blank expression and then, recognition dawning, sat up and exclaimed: 'MacVicar! In the name of Allah! Am I dreaming?'

His wife woke, too. There was a stirring and a leaping out of bed and shouts of laughter at the memory of their hectic party the night before. For an hour we talked and drank coffee, while Angus enjoyed the sight of me in battle dress and I enjoyed the sight of him in his post-party shirt tail. The talk was about Kintyre, about Angus's banking career, about his family and about mine. In adjoining bedrooms Angus's daughter and his balding guest slept on.

At last, unwillingly, I had to go. The convoy was finishing breakfast when I rejoined it. At eight o'clock, on schedule, it started up, and I did my 'thing' as sheepdog on a motor-bike in a happy and reckless spirit which surprised all the drivers. An hour with Angus, clever, sophisticated, but in appearance the perennial schoolboy, had recharged my mental batteries to the point of exhilaration.

Long afterwards Angus told me that his guest that night had been a colonel, one of a number of officers in charge of security during the 'hush-hush' move of the 5th Division from the Middle East to an invasion of Sicily and Italy. When Angus told him of my visit he was scandalised. 'That man,' he said, 'should never have left his convoy. Strictly against regulations. What was his name?'

For the life of him, at that particular moment, Angus couldn't remember.

After the drab emptiness of Persia we looked forward to an evening's leisure in the Arabian Nights city of Baghdad. But Ought-six Kane's dream of 'playing upon the flute and lying with Houris' was unrealised. According to his own account, any houris he did come across were 'scabby auld bints' not fit to be compared with the Ayrshire lassies.

Those of us who prospected for exotic food and drink were equally disappointed. Charlie Cope and I sat on the balcony of a ramshackle restaurant, with the Tigris flowing sullenly beneath. We ordered fish from a tank and sipped glasses of *arak* while waiting for the meal to be served. *Arak* becomes cloudy when mixed with water and has the poisonous sting of a serpent. During a second round we discovered this. It churned in our stomachs and flashed pale signals behind our eyes. We became aware of a foetid smell coming up through the planking from the Tigris. The fish arrived, white, bloated, stinking like a charnel house. We rose, paid our enormous bill after an argument and, metaphorically, shook the dirt and dust of Baghdad off our feet. If this was high life in the Middle East then we preferred the clean asceticism of the desert and the dependable taste of corned beef stew and hot, sweet tea.

We laagered eventually in an area of scrub and sand a few miles outside Damascus, where preparations began for our part in the invasion of Europe's 'soft underbelly'. The MT lines were swathed in barbed wire and guarded night and day, by sentries. This was a vital necessity: the Arabs were skilled and soundless in detaching wheels from vehicles.

One afternoon, enjoying a siesta in my tent, I was aroused by Ought-six Kane. He had returned from Damascus with a truck-load of NAAFI rations, official and unofficial.

'Private Weir,' he said, 'wants tae see ye.'

'Private who?'

'Private Donald Weir, sir. He says him and you were at school thegither.'

'Good God! What's Don Weir doing in Damascus?'

'I'm no' a spaewife, sir.'

'How did you meet him?'

'He saw the truck, wi' the Y67 on it, so he kent I was RSF. "Do you know Captain MacVicar," says he. "Unfortunately I do", says I. "He's my officer." "Good show!" he says. "Tell him I'd like to see him." Then he wrote doon this address.'

An officer is seldom summoned into the presence of a private; but this factor in the situation neither worried nor surprised me, because Don Weir had an original turn of mind and was, in many ways, a law unto himself. I was delighted to be given the chance of meeting him again. I had heard from sources at home that he was in the army—something in Intelligence—and that he had been able to escape from Crete when the island was invaded by Nazi paratroopers. But that he'd gone to ground in Damascus was fresh and exciting news.

Don and his elder brother Jim were old buddies of mine. Often, while at school in Campbeltown, I had been invited for tea to their parents' home outside the town; and on many occasions they had come to join in our hooligan games at the Manse. Jim had become a banker. Don had a flair for writing and had published several books. For what it was worth I'd given him some help with the plot of his first novel, *The Death Stone*, a thriller set on the Dalmatian coast; and after that he'd been a frequent visitor to Southend.

No more welcome guest ever stepped across the threshold of Achnamara. His writing was like himself, lively, full of humour and the joy of life; and he talked exactly as he wrote, often reducing

Jean and me to tears of helpless laughter as he told some outrageous story about mutual friends. Small, slightly stout and slightly
bald, he had an impish grin which could have made a fortune for
him on the stage.

So now he was Private Weir, and he wanted to see me. I wasted
no time in negotiating a twenty-four hour pass.

The address he'd given Ought-six Kane turned out to be that of
a crumbling mansion, surrounded by trees and bushes and set
back from the main road. Two gigantic Senegalese soldiers stood
guard at the gate. They let me through, not without suspicious
scowls, and I parked my jeep under a clump of trees. I began walking along a curving avenue, its gravel almost completely hidden by
weeds. Every ten yards or so I was confronted by more Senegalese
soldiers each apparently about seven feet tall. The phrase 'running
the gauntlet' kept recurring in my mind.

At last I reached stone steps leading up to a pillared entrance.
There I was halted by yet another Senegalese, who pointed his
rifle at me.

'I wish,' I said loudly, camouflaging an utter lack of confidence,
'to see Private Weir.'

His face broke into a white smile. 'Come, dear sir,' he said.

The house, inside, was decrepit. Distempered walls were
blotched. Planks and empty packing-cases lay scattered on echoing
floors. The Senegalese indicated a closed door at the end of a
passage and departed, still smiling, to resume his vigil outside.

I knocked.

'Come in!' roared an unmistakable voice.

I opened the door. Private Weir was sitting back in an easy chair,
a mug of tea in his hand, heavily booted feet propped up comfortably on a table covered with documents. He was wearing khaki
shorts and an open-necked white shirt. His face was almost as
dark as the faces of his bodyguard, though considerably more
lined and haggard. Through an open window came the scent of
mimosa and unceasing insect sounds.

When he saw me he gave a shout, leapt to his feet, slammed his
mug on the table and rushed towards me. 'Angus, my boy, this is
terrific! Sit down, sit down!' Then—'Sulieman!' he yelled, like
the dervish he resembled.

A domesticated Senegalese, unarmed, came to the door.

'Bottle!' commanded Don.

The bottle, when it appeared, was labelled VAT 69, which, as my host explained, was not the Pope's telephone number but the name of a reasonable whisky he'd been able to procure in the NAAFI.

That afternoon, as the hours passed and the level of the liquid in the bottle sank towards zero, we talked as we had never talked before, not about the army or the state of the war but about his family and mine, about Jean and Jock and about other relatives and friends in Southend and Campbeltown. Clinging to civilian topics, we planned great new literary ventures and bellowed with laughter as we savoured their audacity and brilliance. Anxious Senegalese heads appeared from time to time at both door and window, but Don waved them away with lordly gestures and rude words which, he assured me, they didn't understand.

At about six o'clock he got up. 'Now, Angus, we're going out on the town. There's a bathroom through there. Have a wash and a brush-up. When you come back I'll be ready for action.'

Nothing could have appealed to me more than an evening on the town with Don; but anxiety niggled. 'Is it possible?' I said. 'I mean, a private and an officer . . .'

He slapped me on the back, whooping with amusement. 'Don't worry, old boy! All laid on.'

Ten minutes later I returned from the bathroom. I did a double-take. There he stood, dressed in the battle uniform of a major in the artillery and laughing fit to bust. 'Stand to attention, you great oaf! Salute!' he ordered me.

I shook myself sober. 'What the hell's going on? Private Weir? Major Weir? Or what?'

'As you know, Angus, I am a democrat. Private Weir, at your service, sir!'

'But good God, if you're caught wearing a major's uniform . . .'

'Who's going to catch me? Come on, "the rank is but the guinea stamp" . . . all that rot. "On with the dance! Let joy be unconfined!" '

And it was, on that night to remember. We dined and wined at his expense, in the finest restaurant in Damascus. I soon gave up trying to find out what he was and what he did. Good companionship meant more to me than any army regulation. If Don wasn't inclined to worry about a court martial and death at dawn, neither was I.

In the small hours of the morning he took me to a house in the centre of the city. There we mingled with a crowd of English people with whom he appeared to be extremely popular. For our benefit they sang Scots songs with a Cockney accent. For them we sang *Nellie Dean* and *Sweet Lass of Richmond Hill* with a Campbeltown accent.

The dawn was breaking over the minarets when, anxiously scrutinised by the Senegalese guards, I climbed into my jeep and said goodbye to Don at the gate of his mansion. I didn't see him again until the war was over.

What was the truth? Private Weir or Major Weir? Soldier of fortune or secret agent? It may sound incredible, but I still don't know. I have told the story exactly as it happened. Many a time, since then, I have mentioned it to Don, but he always hoods his eyes, bays at me like a hyena and smartly changes the subject.

Nowadays he lives in Sydney, Australia, married to a lovely lady who understands him and appreciates the goodness and essential innocence behind his boisterous humour.

Three years ago he and his Joyce came to Scotland for a holiday. Once again I reminded him of our day together in Damascus.

'We enjoyed it, didn't we?' he grinned.

'You can say that again!'

'Well, isn't that all that matters?'

He spoke a true word. But I have a feeling that somehow, somewhere along the way, Don has been happily pulling my leg.

8

Ought-six Kane—and Monty

WE sailed from Beirut in s.s. *Debrett*. By we I mean the men and loaded vehicles of the 2nd RSF (M.T. Section), along with certain elements of brigade personnel described by my snobbish drivers as 'scruff'.

As the only army officer on board I was OC Troops, a position I relished. For about a fortnight, as we dodged about the Mediterranean waiting to join the main convoy, I was 'Darius, King of Kings', with a luxurious cabin and an attentive steward to myself. I took orders from nobody except, in theory, the captain of the ship. But he was a jovial Englishman with whom I was on the best of terms and who never once interfered with our military regime.

He had no idea of the awful secret I held in my breast.

Before embarkation, we had been reminded, time and time again that our truck-loads must not—repeat not—exceed three tons. This was because the derricks in the *Debrett*, by means of which our vehicles would eventually be lowered into landing craft, were allowed a maximum strain of five tons only. Perhaps in order to ensure that this Board of Trade rule was adhered to it had been laid down that when the trucks were being slung overboard their drivers should accompany them, sitting at the wheel.

On our first morning at sea, somewhere off the Lebanese coast, I was approached by a worried-looking Sergeant Hunter. Ought-six Kane, he said, had something to tell me.

I saw Kane in my cabin. With piratical gusto—and apparent confidence that I would fully approve his actions—he told me a desperate tale. Aboard his truck, now parked in the hold of the ship, he had not only the RSF's NAAFI rations for the invasion of Sicily but the Seaforths' as well.

'Good heavens!' I said. 'Do you mean you pinched them?'

'No, sir. Please try tae understand. I *won* them. The Seaforths got their rations a' richt, but I noticed the silly wee bugger o' a clerk hadna checked them aff in his book, so I tellt him I'd collect theirs as weel as oor ain—bein' in the same brigade, ye ken, an' me wi' such a kindly nature.'

Kindly Kane. It was a contradiction in terms. And yet, even as I prepared to blow my top, he produced from his pockets an assortment of articles which he laid on my bunk. They included razor-blades, cigarettes, shaving-soap and bars of chocolate.

'For yoursel, sir. It was the first thing the lads said tae me when I gi'ed them the good news: "Dinna forget the MTO." Jeest think, sir. When we go ashore on Sicily we'll no' only be the best MT Section in the Division, we'll be the best aff, tae!'

The speech was delivered with a passionate sincerity at variance with the evil in his eyes. Its subtlety was pure genius. Flattering me, titillating my pride in the section, he had made it almost impossible for me to create a row which would deprive us all of a few small comforts on the field of battle. And, the way he put it, our gain had been nobody's loss, not even the Seaforths'.

I struggled with my conscience. Kane had no conscience: that I knew. But in spite of his many 'deeds of shame' I couldn't help being fond of him. In fact, I couldn't help admiring him for having brought off such a magnificent coup. Was I, a small-time poacher of pheasants and salmon, in a position to condemn an operator of such boundless imagination and resource? My conscience capitulated.

But something else had begun to worry me: a matter of logistics.

'Kane,' I said, 'you ought to be shot at dawn.'

'Yes, sir,' he grinned, sure now of my sympathy.

'And your flesh fed to the vultures.'

'They'd find it gey tough, sir.'

'Of that I have no doubt. But have you considered the consequences of what you've done? A double dose of NAAFI rations gives your truck a load of six tons. The truck itself weighs another ton at least. This means that when we come to unload it, a derrick

built for five tons will have to support seven. What if the derrick-
arm or the cable breaks? Remember, you'll be sitting in the
driving-seat.'

'Ach, it's kind o' ye tae consider my safety, sir. But thae derricks
are stronger than ye imagine. A Board o' Trade estimate is aye
conservative. Have nae fear, sir. The MT Section has never failed
yet tae get the rations through, wi' you as oor leader. We'll dae
it again, sir, right under the noses o' the enemy on the shores o'
Sicily!'

By this time I felt I ought to have been standing to attention
singing *Land of Hope and Glory*.

'All right, Kane. That'll do,' I said, ignominiously. 'Leave me
to my grief.'

He departed, aware of his heroic stature, aware that the MTO,
as usual, was like putty in his hands.

I worried about that truck all the way to Sicily. But before we
got there Kane staged another shock for me.

For a time the *Debrett* lay at anchor in the outer harbour at
Alexandria. Our second day there was a Sunday. The captain,
kind and considerate as always, told me that if any of my men
wished to attend church he would send a boat ashore with them.
Privately doubting the wisdom of his offer, I felt it would be
churlish to refuse it. Anyway, it was possible that some Fusiliers,
direct descendants of the Ayrshire Covenanters, might genuinely
want to go to church on the eve of our invasion of Sicily. A few of
them might die in the battle. In such a case, I should always
blame myself if I denied them the benefit of religion during their
last few days on earth. But, knowing my troops, I had the feeling
that churchgoing, for the majority, wouldn't be the most powerful
magnet for a few hours' leave ashore.

Arrangements were made that the boat, in charge of a ship's
officer, should leave the *Debrett* at ten o'clock in the morning and
return from Alexandria not later than three o'clock in the afternoon. When I asked my men how many of them would like to
join the party a profusion of hands shot into the air, among them,
inevitably, the claw-like talons of Ought-six Kane.

'Very good,' I said. 'Sergeant Hunter will go with you and make sure that you all do go to church. According to the letter of the law we're not supposed to leave the ship until we reach our final destination, so remember—this is a special privilege you're being given. Strict security must be maintained. When the service is over you may have a meal and a stroll around the town until three o'clock. But that's all. If anybody steps out of line, if anybody gets drunk or risks contracting VD, there will be hell to pay.'

I was rewarded by smiles and nods of the utmost innocence.

Holiness shone from the wolfish face of Ought-six Kane. I saw him shake his head sorrowfully at the lack of trust displayed by his beloved officer.

The captain and I stood by the rail as the boat moved off towards the distant quays. Smart in their tropical kit, the Fusiliers waved up to us.

'Fine lot of fellows you have. Well disciplined, too.' The captain was an idealist. 'They deserve a break.'

'Sure,' I answered, leaving unsaid my fervent prayer that they would all return unscathed.

At ten past three, to my relief, I saw the boat coming back. A quick count of heads, as it approached the ship, seemed to indicate that nobody was absent.

Then I saw Sergeant Hunter's face.

'Kane,' I said, as he climbed aboard. 'Kane's missing?'

'Yes, sir. We searched for him everywhere. We had a meal at a restaurant. Afterwards he left us to go to the lavatory. We never saw him again.'

This was a facer. I was troubled not only about Kane's future but also about my own. Losing a man in such circumstances might lead eventually to a court martial.

'Well,' I said to Sergeant Hunter, 'seems there's only one thing we can do. Go ashore and hand the matter over to the military police.'

Hunter nodded, reluctantly.

Some of my other drivers were listening. I think it was Darroch who said: 'Maybe you should wait, sir. Just for a wee while. I'm thinking Kane won't let you down.'

'Wait for what, Darroch? He'd need a helicopter to get to us here.'

'Or a dhow, sir.'

'A dhow?'

'Yes, sir. There's scores of them in the harbour, all for hire.'

The idea gave us new hope. Joy might still be wrested from despair. 'Right,' I said. 'We'll give him until four o'clock.'

I put the situation to the captain. If the worst happened, and Kane didn't show up in the next hour, he promised to let me have a boat.

Meanwhile Hunter, Darroch and the rest congregated on the foredeck, looking towards the harbour, where dhow sails flickered in and out among the motionless mass of shipping, white gadflies in the sun. Presently I joined them.

At about half-past three a dhow was observed in the distance, sail fully set. Its course was erratic, but in the main it appeared to be moving in our direction.

I sent for my binoculars. Focusing them carefully, I was able to see two men in the dhow. One, in native garb, was kneeling amidships in an attitude of prayer. The other stood erect at the tiller, sunlight gleaming on a bare and partially bald head.

'It's Kane, drunk,' I said. 'He's taken over.'

In great sweeps and lurches the dhow came towards us. At every turn its gun'le dipped below the surface of the water. When it reached a position about a hundred yards away we realised it was slowly filling and sinking. The cries of its Arab owner, calling upon Allah, floated up to us. Ought-six Kane was concentrating on his steering. The water was rising towards his knees, but he seemed unaware of this and stood as straight and steady as a boy on a burning deck.

Closer came the dhow. Deeper and deeper it floundered. As it slewed alongside the *Debrett* the Arab climbed half-way up the mast and succeeded in bringing down the sail. The water was now lapping Kane's waist; but, hand firm on the tiller, he ignored his plight.

Aboard ship, a few watchers—but only a few—were enjoying the bizarre spectacle. Tears of laughter in his eyes, the captain ordered his men to put a derrick into action. A small boat was launched, a great hook lowered.

But Kane remained master of the situation. He saw us lining the rails. He saw the small boat approaching. He heard the clank of the derrick and caught sight of the hook coming down.

'Women and children first!' he shouted. He glanced up at me and raised his free hand in salute. 'Goodbye, sir,' he called. 'The captain aye goes doon wi' his ship!'

The Arab, shrieking, leapt overboard. Stern first the dhow slid under. Straight-backed, still at the salute, Kane slid under, too.

Fortunately, there was no danger. The seamen in the small boat attached the derrick hook to the forepart of the dhow. Then, using lifebuoys, they rescued Kane and the Arab.

We watched, fascinated, as the dhow was hauled up out of the water, allowed to drip for a minute or two and then lowered on to an even keel again. The Arab, well rewarded, resumed command of his ill-used craft and quickly sailed off towards the safety of Alexandria.

Kane, now feigning unconsciousness, was carried aboard and taken to the sick bay.

He and I would, before long, have a confrontation. In the meantime his mates were happy, the captain and his crew were happy—and I was happy, too.

What passed between Kane and myself on the following day is not for publication. He ought to have been punished with the utmost severity. I am ashamed to confess he got away with it. I did, of course, lash him with my tongue; but I knew that a verbal dressing-down—from me—meant nothing to him. My words were water. His back was even oilier than a duck's. Half-an-hour after the interview ended, as I sat in my cabin recovering from the ordeal, he arrived at the door, smiling in the friendliest way, and presented me with more goodies from the Aladdin's cave which was his truck.

As Sergeant Hunter said, afterwards: 'I know, sir. What can you do? When it comes to the bit he's one of the best soldiers we have.'

But that overloaded truck still worried me.

In the dark hours before we landed in Sicily (10 July, 1943) we

lay off shore in a position south of Syracuse. We heard the
American aircraft go in, towing gliders which carried our 1st Air
Landing Brigade. Not until morning did we discover that most of
the gliders had been cast off too early by the American pilots and
that, as a result, scores of British soldiers had been needlessly
drowned.

Two hours before dawn, the 2nd RSF and the remainder of
the 5th Division went ashore in the northern corner of the Gulf
of Noto. When daylight came we began to unload our vehicles
and join them on the beachhead.

The fireworks occurring in the green and yellow countryside of
Sicily, reinforced by a few sinister puffs from Mount Etna, were
fascinating to watch, but we could spend little time admiring them.
The unloading operation occupied most of our attention.

In spite of a groundswell caused by strong winds the previous
day it went reasonably well, unhampered by attacks either from
enemy guns on shore or from enemy planes in the sky. We learnt
later that this was due to the superb air cover organised by the
RAF. As the landing craft plied back and forth from ship to
beach, I felt a burden of anxiety gradually lifting. But Kane and
his NAAFI truck remained in the hold. They would be the last to
come up, and not until they were safely in the landing craft could
I utter a sigh of relief.

The time came. The double slings on the derrick cable were
adjusted on the wheels. Kane climbed into his seat.

'Get out of there,' I said.

He cocked an eyebrow, preparing to argue.

'Get out! That's an order, Kane.'

He got out.

Aware of the instruction that drivers should sit in their vehicles
during unloading, the ship's officer in charge started to say
something.

'The driver's sick,' I snapped at him. 'Get the truck out!'

He looked surprised, then shrugged and signalled up to the
winchman.

The derrick clanked. The cable tautened. There was a creaking
and a groaning. The truck began to rise, bobbing horribly like a
grilse on a light rod.

Kane and I hurried on deck. The derrick arm seemed to bend. The winchman looked puzzled as he turned on full power.

The truck emerged from the hold. It hung high in the air. The winchman moved a lever and it swung gently over the rails and out above the landing craft. It continued to bob and curtsey. The cable twanged.

'Say your prayers, Kane,' I suggested.

He complied. Behind me his gangster voice whispered: 'Gentle Jesus, meek and mild, look upon a little child . . .'

The truck began to descend. Down it went, slowly, heavily. Sparks flew—maybe from the derrick engine, maybe from the tortured cable: I cannot tell. Then suddenly, thankfully, it was in the landing craft, among a huddle of other vehicles. The slings were loosed.

In silence Kane and I spared each other a smile. Our major troubles were over. The 2nd RSF (MT Section) was landing in Sicily in good shape and in good heart.

About a year later, at Anzio, Kane was in a party bringing rations to a company in an exposed position. He was struck and killed by shrapnel from a German mortar.

When we broke out of Anzio and captured Rome—and made political obeisance to our US allies by letting them in first— Sergeant Hunter was accidently killed by brawling Americans.

Kane was a 'villain', but a villain who never, if he could help it, allowed his villainy to interfere with the well-being of his friends. Hunter was an honest soldier, disciplined and straight, who did his duty faithfully by all ranks. Each, in his own way, increased for others the joy of living. I missed them both, more than I can tell.

In Sicily—and, later, in Italy—we were part of the Eighth Army, under the command of General Sir Bernard Law Montgomery, otherwise known as Monty. His name was legendary long before we joined his circus.

We had heard tales about his unorthodox views on military dress, his implacable discipline, his keen sense of the dramatic.

A replacement officer who'd joined us in Syria had been with

Southern Command in England while Monty was in charge. To everyone's horror, he told us, the general had initiated a PT session for staff officers each morning at 6 o'clock. As a rule this took the form of a cross-country run, in which Monty himself joined with cold-bath vigour. On one occasion a certain colonel was missing from parade. Afterwards Monty sent for him.

'Not on PT this morning?'

'I was a bit under the weather, sir.'

'Why?'

'Well, you see, sir, we had a party last night, A farewell party for an officer who is leaving us. A tradition in the mess, sir.'

'I see. You will be having another farewell party tonight. Yours. Good morning.'

We treasured the story about his departure from England to take command of the Eighth Army in North Africa, following the death of General Gott in a plane crash. Churchill accompanied him to the airfield. As they sat together in the back of the staff car Monty waxed sadly philosophical about the unfortunate quirks of war, about the trials of a commander suddenly uprooted from orthodox military routine in order to wage great battles against a brilliant opponent.

Churchill tried to comfort him. 'You'll be all right, Monty. You have a great deal of experience . . .'

'Oh, I'm not referring to myself, sir.' The voice was slightly pained. 'I'm thinking about Rommel.'

As the Sicilian campaign developed we wondered how we'd get along with this slightly eccentric boss. In the event most of us learned to trust and admire him, and his glamorous operation orders, some containing the unusual information that we were about to 'hit the enemy for six', had us walking ten feet tall. Even if we didn't hit the enemy for six—as frequently happened—we were grateful to somebody who thought we could, and this, I believe, made us keener soldiers.

A few of his high-ranking colleagues were inclined to cock a snook at Monty, regarding him as a brash upstart and vulgar showman. We, the common soldiery, enjoyed having a leader who was brash and a showman. At the back of our minds was the conviction that Monty was behaving as he did for a special purpose—to give his soldiers that conceit in themselves which is required for success in battle.

We also got the idea that he was interested not only in brigadiers and colonels but also in the lowliest corporals and privates. His order that all ranks in the Eighth Army must know exactly where they were at any given time—and why—gave officers many a headache; but it was obviously good for morale and we approved of it. We liked his published opinion that it was courage and disciplined team-work that gained victories, not drill displays, blanco-ed equipment and polished boots.

Soon after our arrival in Sicily we had proof of his mettle. Men in the back areas, working in a humid climate, discarded all possible clothing. Some even took to wearing wide-brimmed Sicilian straw hats. Monty made no effort to curb this move towards maximum physical comfort. One day, however, as he was being conveyed in an open car towards the front, he saw a truck approaching with a soldier in the driver's seat apparently naked and wearing a silk top hat.

'As the lorry passed me,' he writes in his *Memoirs*, 'the driver leant out from his cab and took off his hat to me with a sweeping and gallant gesture. I just roared with laughter. However, while I was not particular about dress so long as the soldiers fought well and won our battles, I at once decided there were limits. When I got back to my headquarters I issued the only order I ever issued about dress in the Eighth Army; it read as follows: "Top hats will not be worn in the Eighth Army." '

This was the kind of leader we understood and respected: somebody dedicated to his job who could also betray humanity and a sense of humour. We knew plenty of generals who were brilliant on paper. It was thrilling to have one who was brilliant in action.

I believe Monty to be a naturally sensitive and retiring man who, in order to inspire trust and fighting fervour in his troops, deliberately schemed to make himself into a 'character'. He and Ought-six Kane had a lot in common. They even looked like each other.

One day, near Lentini in Italy, I was standing at a road fork, my motorbike propped up behind me, guiding a long column of vehicles on to the proper route. The operation was going well. I wanted it over quickly, however, because the village through which the trucks and carriers were approaching was being intermittently shelled.

Suddenly a long gap appeared in the column. The sun was in my eyes, but I could see that the vehicle causing the hold-up was a jeep. It came rolling downhill at an infuriatingly slow pace, and I started to yell at its driver. My language contained every swear-word I could remember.

Then, out of the glare, the jeep emerged only a few yards away from me. I saw that beside the driver there sat an officer wearing a black beret.

'Get cracking, you stupid, misbegotten son of a so-and-so!' I shouted at him. 'Don't you realise there's a war on?'

Then I choked into silence. The officer was Monty. Instinctively, though unnecessarily in an area of war, I sprang to a salute.

He grinned in a wolfish way. As he passed he waved his right hand, two fingers raised and parted, in Churchillian salute.

Our stay in the region of Lentini was, for me, punctuated by several more unnerving incidents.

One day the MT Section laagered in a vineyard, one part of which, in a series of walled terraces about two to three feet high, rippled down a long slope into a valley. I failed to realise that the gateway through which we had entered was also the only exit and parked an ammunition truck slap across it.

We were enjoying a lunch of biscuits, cheese and onions when an enemy shell burst just outside the gate. Shrapnel thudded against the ammunition truck, its camouflage net caught fire and the ammunition inside began to explode.

How none of us was killed is a mystery. Bullets zipped among the trees; mortar bombs went off with terrible crashes, metal splinters tearing at the vine leaves.

Scores of my vehicles were trapped, the majority of them loaded with ammunition, and I had a despairing picture of them all being set alight, one after another, and the place erupting in a huge, Etna-like explosion, with us in the middle of it.

Our only way of escape was through the valley far below. Could we possibly drive our trucks down and across the walled terraces?

As I might have expected, it was Ought-six Kane who led the charge and, by his example, encouraged the others to follow. While a continuous firework display went on in the main area of the vineyard above, his NAAFI truck leapt, nose-dived, bounced, crashed, teetered on two wheels, righted itself, roared, screamed and eventually stopped, upright and virtually undamaged, on the valley floor. In a few minutes, as this cross between a Donnybrook Fair and the Badminton Horse Trials came to an end, it was joined by the remainder of the transport.

A number of springs were broken, two of the drivers had bruised hands. Otherwise, not counting the truck at the gate, we were intact, with no casualties. Sergeant Hunter and I, faces black with smoke, our battledress stained with mud and leaf-mould, exchanged words of thankfulness.

That evening I was summoned to Battalion HQ. The CO didn't even mention the shambles of the afternoon. He told me that promotions had come through and handed me my third pips.

Later in the night the MT Section formally congratulated the MTO. They didn't give a damn for my new rank as captain, but it was a fine excuse for a semi-official booze-up. Toasts were drunk in NAAFI whisky and in vino liberated from a house in the valley by Ought-six Kane. The wine was slightly harsh, but to us it tasted good. We had just faced disaster together and, thanks to God and Kane, escaped without serious loss. It was exactly the kind of soil in which comradeship flourishes.

In the same area, a few days after our vineyard adventure, I sat one morning in my jeep in a small clearing in a wood, checking spare parts lists. We were only about a mile from the front, but all was peaceful in the green glade. Fusilier McKinlay tinkered with the jeep's carburettor and Fusilier Molloy, the section cook, brewed up tea on a smokey paraffin stove. The rest of the MT were some distance away, shacked up in a denser part of the wood.

Molloy was from Glasgow, stout, sweaty and with the easy-going habits of army cooks. He was not—and never would be—a soldier. The arts of war were of no interest to him whatever. But despite his unpromising appearance he was a good cook and we did our best to hide him away in trucks and cookhouses, safe from prying COs and adjutants who might suddenly demand his presence on parade or ask some question demanding a military answer.

I heard a vehicle approaching along a track in the wood but paid small attention. It would be Darroch, I imagined, with the water truck. About an hour ago he had been sent back to a nearby village to replenish his tank.

Then McKinlay froze over the carburettor, whistling through his teeth. I looked up and saw a staff car entering the clearing, a flag fluttering on the bonnet. It stopped. Out of it stepped Monty, with a map.

I dropped my papers hurriedly and approached him, realising immediately that he was on one of his test runs, finding out if his orders were being passed down to the meanest ranks.

He spread the map on the bonnet of his car, gave me a tight smile and said: 'Where are we?'

'There, sir.' I pointed.

'Good. All your men equally well informed?'

'Yes, sir.'

He directed eagle eyes at McKinlay. My temporary batman was mentally alert and had been specially briefed for such an occasion. But to my dismay Monty's glance passed over him and came to rest on Molloy, still doggedly engaged in brewing up.

'Come here!' Monty called to him.

Molloy shambled forward, brows furrowed, a puzzled look on his broad, pale face. It was the first time any officer—except, of course, the MTO—had spoken to him for months.

'Name?' snapped Monty.

In a hoarse tenor Molloy gave the requisite details.

'You know exactly where we are?'

'Yes, sir.'

'Then show me. On this map.'

Until now Molloy had been unaware of our visitor's identity. Now I saw recognition spark quick astonishment from his eyes. He stared at the lean, tanned face surmounted by the beret.

'Show me! On the map,' repeated Monty, with a hint of irritation.

I said a quiet prayer. The previous day I had given my troops a short run-down on our operations and, using a big map, had indicated our present whereabouts. Had Molloy been interested enough to absorb such information?

With apparent reluctance he transferred his fascinated attention from a face to a map. Then, slowly, he raised a smoke-grimed, grease-stained finger and brought it down with force.

'We're jeest aboot here, sir.' Then, looking up anxiously, he added: 'Are ye lost?'

Monty flicked at the black smudge now showing on his map. He didn't smile, but there was a sudden bright twinkle in his eyes. 'Excellent, Molloy. No, I'm not lost. Merely checking.'

'I was makin' tea for the MTO. Wad ye like a cup?'

'Good idea. But it must be quick.'

'Sure, sir. The can's jeest on the boil.'

The general folded up his map and turned to me. 'Remarkable,' he said, then barked a question: 'You trust your men?'

'Yes, sir.'

'So do I. Helps a lot.'

Molloy came with two cracked enamel mugs full of a steaming liquid resembling tea. One he gave to Monty. The other he presented to Monty's driver.

Monty took a couple of sips, handed back the mug and said: 'Thank you. Now I must be off!'

His driver gulped, dropped his mug on the ground, started up and drove off. I was left wondering how far Monty really did trust his men. For instance, what would have been his reaction if Molloy hadn't, with unexpected brilliance, turned up trumps?

'Well, Molloy, what do you think of him?' I said.

'A fine man, sir. But I wish tae hell him an' his driver hadna wasted a' that tea!'

The next top brass I met during the war was German. It happened in Lübeck, in May, 1945, when the confused fighting for Europe had come to an end.

The CO—Jock Maxwell—sent for me. 'We have captured Field
Marshall Earhard Milch. He has expressed a curious wish that
before being sent to a prison camp he should be taken round the
docks in one of those long, flat-bottomed harbour boats you were
telling me about last night. See to it, will you?'

I was aware of the reasoning behind his order. The craft he
referred to had outboard motors; they were transport, of a kind.
In theory, therefore, the obvious choice to carry out such a
commission was the MTO.

Assisted by Jack Hibbett, now my top sergeant, I liberated one
of the flat-bottomed boats, got the motor running to my satisfaction and essayed a practice run among the desolate quays. At
home, in Southend, I had frequently handled outboard motor-boats
but never one as awkward and recalcitrant as this. Its extreme
narrowness and its length—all of 20 feet, I reckoned—made it as
unmanageable as a rogue elephant, and Hibbett and I spent a
long time yawing about the harbour like Ought-six Kane in his
dhow at Alexandria.

Finally, however, I got the hang of it and told the CO I was
ready for Field Marshall Milch.

Escorted by Drum-Major Guthrie and a military policeman, he
marched stiffly down the pier, a big chunky man, uniform tight
across his chest. His broad, clean-shaven face, pitted and murky
brown, was scarred with *mensur* marks. It was expressionless,
like a death-mask. He climbed down the steps and sat amidships,
his escort behind him. He faced me in the stern, back erect and
stiff, arms folded. A monocle dangled from his neck, but he
didn't wear it.

I started the motor and asked him, in pigeon German, where
he would like to go. He stared over my shoulder and made no
reply.

Guthrie said: 'The auld bugger's in a dwam, sir. Micht as weel
tak' him oot tae sea an' droon him!'

'The way I handle this boat, Guthrie, we may all be drowned in
the next few minutes!'

He grinned at me, the ends of his waxed moustache cockily in
the air. 'We never died a winter yet, did we, sir?'

We cast off, I let the outboard motor drop into the water and for about an hour we moved carefully in and out among the extensive docks, passing idle ships, some at anchor, some tied up at deserted quays. Most of them looked derelict.

Milch sat heavy and still, empty eyes turned in my direction but never meeting mine. I felt pity for him. His dreams were at an end. Guthrie and I, due for demob within a few months, ours were just beginning.

I don't know why, but his stone face made me think not of Monty, his conqueror, but of King Darius.

9

A Touch of Nature

Southend is principally a farming community. In World War I, because many farmers and farmers' sons were Territorials, it supplied a great many fighting men. When the war ended the returning warriors were given a warm welcome and a slap-up dinner at the inn. In World War II, agricultural workers being reserved, Southend's quota of service men was small, consisting mainly of volunteers. Boskers (Lt Col Hamish Taylor, MC, TD) and a few others (including myself) came home to a parish which, while thankful that hostilities were over, was disinclined to show much interest in what had now become history. A quick whip-round was made, and a retired solicitor came secretly to our doors, thrusting at each of us a £5 note. This, he gave us to understand, was in gratitude for our heroic exploits. But now, life having returned to normal, he inferred that the sooner they were forgotten the better.

We thoroughly agreed with him, and most of us, I think, donated our £5 to the fund required for adding further names to the local war memorial.

For me, being home again with Jean and Jock, in daily contact with 'the Manse folk' and other neighbours, was more than sufficient reward for six years of physical and spiritual discomfort. After the malarial heat, the desert sand and the cordite-smelling ruins of wartime, the freshness of Southend was like paradise regained. After the chaos and the killing, after the loss of Archie and of many friends, the quiet of the green countryside was balm on mental scars. For some weeks after my demob I took time off to absorb it all.

I visited the old bridge above the Minister's Lynn. Long ago it had gleamed yellow, painted annually for the shooters, with their dogs and guns and vivacious ladies. Now its moss-grown planks were soft and slippery, and as I looked over into the Con's brown water I took care to lean lightly on the handrail.

It was so silent on the bridge that I could hear a pheasant calling on the moor above the planting and a collie barking near Kilblaan farm as the cows were brought in for milking.

The smell of winter was strong. It came from mole-heaps on the damp verges of the burn, from sycamore leaves trapped in foamy eddies, from a turnip-field beyond the hedge, from wood-smoke curling like a limp banner from a chimney in the Manse.

Psychologists describe our sense of smell as a root cause of nostalgia. They may be right.

I saw the rusty iron beam close under the bridge and remembered a winter's day when I had swung across it, hand over hand, to display my courage and agility to Archie and Willie and Rona. I could still feel the cold of the iron and the slipperiness of the paint on it. I could still feel desperate tiredness invading my arms and the horror of reaching a point of no return, with chill water and sharp rocks fifteen feet below. I still caught my breath as in memory I rushed at the final span and missed my grip and fell—luckily into a sandy shallow which damaged nothing but my pride.

Rona, aged 3, had laughed until the tears ran down her chubby cheeks, imagining I had done it for her benefit. For Archie and Willie the big brother image was sadly dented.

Another day I stood with John Cameron in the lee of his red-roofed equipment store. Black, swollen clouds were gathering in the sou'-west, and the wind was beginning to whine among the crags at the river-mouth. I knew that within an hour Southend would be blanketed in driving rain.

John was the salmon-fisher, lean and brown, with sea-wise eyes accustomed to gauging distances and wrists toughened by a life-time's oaring. He was also a farmer, but the sea was his first love.

In May he laid his nets in the tide-run outside the estuary of the Con. The law compelled him to lift them finally at the end of September, when, in theory, the hen-fish and their cavaliers no longer run upstream for the spawning. But on that harsh winter's day, one salmon at least was ignoring theory. We saw him leap just beyond the estuary bar, a taut, streamlined bow of energy.

John sighed, vainly covetous. He said: 'He knows it's going to rain. He's waiting out there to come upstream on the flood.'

Long ago, before the war, John had talked to me about the mystery of the salmon. Now I persuaded him to talk about it again. I believed that for a soldier sated with evidence of man's inhumanity to man and determined to retrieve a countryman's patient ethos, it might be good therapy.

The smolt, John said, is hatched in the burn, where he lives and feeds for two years. By then he looks like a tiny trout, less than six inches long. But already he has grown a protective garment of sea-scales, and in the spring a longing stirs in his blood for the salty ocean he has never known.

With his companions he begins to swim with the stream—beneath the bridges, down the scurrying shallows, past John's equipment store and out beyond the bar. Finally, flicking along the weakening eddies of fresh water, he moves out and down into the rocky shades of the Atlantic.

For two, three, perhaps four years he is lost to man. But during this time, as John told me, he feeds greedily, first on minute fish, small shrimps and crustaceans, then on the rich herring-shoals. From a shivering, two-ounce smolt he grows into a sleek ocean fighter of anything up to forty pounds, silver-flanked, white bellied, the glow of reddish spots on his brown hog-back.

Then again there is a stirring in his blood. Back he swims with the others along the undersea paths he used as a smolt. Threatened by sharks, porpoises and seals, he swims unerringly along the sea-trail imprinted on his ancestral memory.

Hundreds of miles he travels, thrusting and swerving, impelled by his tireless black tail, until at last, with rising excitement, he feels the movement of fresh water—the water of the very river in which he was born. Beyond the bar he leaps in ecstacy, shedding the sea-lice on his body as he waits for a flood to give him elbow-room in the river. It is late summer, and John sees the silver acrobat and his hopes are high.

But though others may be caught, the big salmon circumnavigates the net in a swirl of flood-water. Beside him there appears a hen-fish, broadbeamed with eggs.

The flood subsides and the burn becomes pellucid and quiet. But they journey on, the cock-fish and his mate, eating nothing, heeding nothing in the tremendous urge of their purpose. On and on they go to where the water widens into a sandy pool—the one, perhaps, beneath the shooters' bridge. There the female settles down among the sand, while the male spins round in eager circles, waiting.

On successive days in winter the hen-fish emits dangling clouds of eggs. Each time, fighting off excited rivals for her nearness, the big salmon covers them with his milt.

Months later, in the spring, drained of feeling, emaciated with hunger and preyed on by clinging fungus, they drift downstream— the kelts, the exhausted ones, seeking new energy from the salts of the ocean.

This was John's story. Years later I was talking on the same subject to my brother, Kenneth, at his manse in Perthshire. He told me a strange thing. When, as a result of a hydro-electric scheme, the waters of the Lyon became mingled with those of the Tay, surprised Perthshire fishermen began to find the Tay filled with Glen Lyon salmon. According to this evidence it must be the water, not the exact geographical location, that the big fish recognises.

I remember another afternoon, just after the war, when my room in Achnamara became hot and stuffy with cigarette smoke and the hero of a story I was writing got himself into an impossible situation. I packed up the typewriter, therefore, donned a windcheater and waterproof trousers and went outside to clear my head in the first of the December gales.

I tramped across the shore and climbed Dunaverty Rock. On its summit, ninety feet above the sea, I gulped down lungfuls of the battering, salty wind.

Far to the left I saw Ailsa Craig and the outline of the Ayrshire coast, to the right the round grey hills of Antrim, secretive in the winter haze. Below me the sea curled and frothed and leaped, flinging its spray so high that sometimes it struck my face and ran down my chin like sweat.

Dismissing the problems of my hero, I thought instead about

this turf-coated lump of Old Red Sandstone, formed of pebbles cemented together by sand and silt while the earth cooled.

As boys, accompanied by a University professor, Archie and Willie and I had searched its crannies for fossil impressions of the trilobites, small extinct shellfish which, three hundred million years ago, were the highest form of life. Guided by our mentor we had actually found some, though to us the specimens appeared disappointingly vague and undramatic.

Afterwards he had talked about the sea.

Like the trilobites, he told us, every living creature has developed from a spot of protoplasm in the primeval ocean, ourselves included. When our remote ancestors came ashore to begin a life on land they possessed a circulatory system in which the fluid was, in fact, the water of the sea.

We had gaped at this extraordinary information, but more was to come. Even today, according to our companion, the blood in our veins—as in the veins of every fish, reptile, amphibian and mammal—combines sodium, potassium and calcium in about the same proportions as in sea water. Similarly, our lime-hardened skeletons are a heritage from the calcium-rich ocean of millions of years ago.

I stood there for a long time, remembering the words of the wise man and enjoying the taste of the sea as it struck the rock and exploded upwards in flying confusion. More and more I became aware that under the icy surface of that same sea rich life waited in the warmer depths for the magic touch of spring. Words came into my head:

> A thousand ages in Thy sight
> Are like an evening gone;
> Short as the watch that ends the night
> Before the rising sun.

In face of a plan and a purpose evolving through three hundred million years, my war and post-war anxieties began to seem like very small wrinkles in the graph of time.

The therapy was working. A sense of proportion was coming back.

Jean loves all natural things. Robins, ferrets, ponies, dogs and cats —especially cats—display joy on meeting her and before long have her completely in their power. Jock is the same. Southend had always given them full scope for their love affairs.

At sunrise on a calm, cold winter's morning the seals come up on the rocks close to Achnamara. They sprawl and puff and stretch —brown seals and grey—and when Jean or Jock whistle they turn to look, immediately curious.

What always strikes me about a seal is that when it stretches, balancing on its belly with head and tail arched upwards, it has the appearance of a gigantic bird. To me, this resemblance is proof of the theory of evolution. I like to imagine that the seal—which is, of course, a mammal—has reached the half-way stage between a ceolocanth lurking blindly in some deep-sea cavern and an eagle soaring in the sunny sky.

Grey seals are friendly in a way that is almost human. One day, when Jock was about nine years old, he found a furry white calf playing alone at the bottom of a clear sea-pool, curiously turning over shells and stones with its small hands. As I sat by my typewriter at the window, watching instead of working, I saw them beginning to talk to each other. Next thing I knew my son was coming in at the front gate with the calf heaving and puffing behind him.

Much to Jock's disappointment we returned the baby to the sea. We found difficulty in explaining to him that in the long run it would be much happier as a seal than as a human being.

Ian, the Achnamara cat, was convinced he was a human being.

His mother was a thoroughbred, the Lady Susan, his father a roving tramp known in the parish as Old Donald. This probably accounted for contrasting elements in his character and appearance. The impeccable cleanliness, for example, compared with occasional bouts of swashbuckling violence; the underside so white and sleek compared with his main covering of shaggy grey.

One afternoon, the Lady Susan and I were alone together in the house, Jean being at a Guild Committee meeting and Jock at school. Suddenly, to my horror, I realised that in the armchair opposite mine she was beginning to have kittens. I scooped her up, along with the first of her brood, and carried her out by the back door. Ian was born half way to the garage, falling with a plop on the gravel at my feet.

For me it was a traumatic experience, and when Jean and Jock returned home that evening they were forcibly reminded that the Lady Susan was *their* cat and that it ought to have been their job, not mine, to attend her in a gynaecological crisis.

From that day Ian purred with a determined vigour which saved him from the usual fate of unwanted kittens. Having been 'dressed' at an early age, he went on to enjoy a gentleman's life, the life to which his mother's aristocratic lineage so well fitted him.

During the day he dozed by the fire, while I laboured at my desk to earn his keep. I am, in Beverley Nichols's once fashionable phrase, non-F; but Ian and I lived together amicably enough. From me he expected none of the demonstrative affection given him by Jean and Jock. If he wished to leave the room, however, he was more than willing to inform me, knowing that he could depend on my co-operation in a slow and dignified exit.

At one time Jean kept her cats shut in at night. Later she discovered that full feline health depends on their being free to move about in the nocturnal air. After dark, therefore, Ian was put in the garage, where he had a bed; but the door was left partially open, and he spent a lot of time in the surrounding fields. (That leaving the garage door open in a seaside environment caused rusty stains on the car and the lawn-mower was unimportant to Jean and Jock compared with Ian's well-being. I remained in a sulky minority of one.)

There was no need for Ian to hunt. He was well fed on fish, red meat and milk with the chill taken off. (Oh, yes, carefully and regularly the chill was taken off!) But as I enjoyed my golf, so he seemed to enjoy his chosen sport, and we often found the results on the doorstep—field mice, rats, rabbits, even an occasional weasel.

Few cats will tackle a weasel, a cunning and ferocious fighter. The tougher the opponent, however, the better Ian liked it. After a successful night he used to stalk into my work-room with an air of aloof but unmistakable satisfaction, in much the same way as my golfing friends John Burgoyne and Alan Lamont come into the clubhouse after a good round in the monthly medal.

Before he learned road-sense Ian was struck by a car outside Achnamara front gate. His head was injured, and we despaired of his life. But after three days he was tempted to swallow a morsel of fish, and from that moment he began to recover, though the sight of one eye had permanently gone.

The accident made no difference to his skill as a hunter. On the other hand, as an interesting invalid, he played on Jean and Jock's sympathy even more cunningly than before. Now, instead of the hearthrug, he passed most evenings curled up in the lap of his choice, purring in smug contentment. Once he essayed to pinch my armchair, no doubt with a view to making it his own. In this case, however, I stuck up courageously for my rights, despite the fact that my nearest and dearest failed to offer me even token support.

Ian grew old along with us. As he approached the age of 20, he became deaf—probably a delayed result of his accident—and bad teeth made eating difficult. We were coming to the sad conclusion that he would have to be put down when the situation was unexpectedly resolved for us. One morning a neighbour found him on the road, some distance from the house. He had been run over by a lorry which, as we guessed, he had failed to hear.

By now Jock was working in Glasgow, and Jean refused to go near the mangled body. So, as at his birth, I officiated at his death. I buried him deep on the shore, the place of many a happy hunting.

This happened on the morning the Tories came into power in June, 1970. It was a pity Ian didn't live to see the day. He was a true blue Tory, if ever there was one.

For Jean and Jock there are two inexcusable criminals. One is a singer who goes flat or off tune. The other, predictably, is someone cruel to animals. The story told in Southend about the 'last' fox at the Mull of Kintyre fills them with horror.

The Goings is the local name of a long path leading up from the shore near Borgadale to the high crags at the Mull lighthouse. At one stage it winds along the sheer cliff-face, four hundred feet above the sea. In places, when John Cameron and I walked it just after the war, it narrowed to a width of about eighteen inches. It is rumoured that nowadays it has become impassable, owing to landslides, but nothing would ever tempt me to go near it again in order to make sure.

Fifty years ago, however, it was in regular use, mainly by shepherds, gamekeepers and rabbit-trappers. Once, for a drunken bet, a young farmer tried to ride his horse from one end to the other. All went well until he came to the narrows. By then he had sobered up, and as he looked far down at the crawling sea he lost his nerve. The horse completed the journey. Its rider had to be rescued from the cliff, shivering with cold and terror.

Towards the end of last century only one fox—a vixen—remained alive in the area. The Duke of Argyll's foxhunter saw her often, slinking through the heather, always out of range of his gun. When he followed her track he found to his amazement that it led on to the Goings at its highest level. As he watched from the cliff-top he saw her skirt a protuding boulder and waited for her to reappear on the path beyond. He waited in vain. Puzzled, he climbed down and searched the Goings from end to end but found no sign of her.

Next day he watched from a different angle and, using a spyglass, witnessed an almost incredible sight. A few yards beyond the boulder a hawthorn grew in the cliff-face, just below the level of the path. Down on to the bush the vixen jumped. Then, using teeth and paws to maintain balance, she scrambled along it and disappeared into a hollow hideout in the cliff itself.

The foxhunter made a cruel plan. One afternoon, while the vixen was away from her den, he crawled along the Goings and loosened the roots of the hawthorn. When the vixen returned in the evening it gave way beneath her and she fell to her death, down and down on to the rocks and the seaweed and into the sea.

During World War II the foxes returned to Kintyre. But now they are again being banished by the guns of farmers anxious about their lambs—and their poultry.

The view from the high crags of the Mull is magnificent. Only eleven miles away across the North Channel lie Torr Head and Fairhead on the Irish coast, with Rathlin Island in the foreground.

On a clear day the Giant's Causeway can be seen on the horizon.

Visitors to Southend are always told that from the Mull they can see five kingdoms. The kingdom of Scotland, of course; the kingdom of Ireland; the kingdom of England in the shape of the Cumberland hills, and the kingdom of Man, a distant smudge in the Irish Sea.

'But you said five kingdoms?'

'Sure. There's also the kingdom of Heaven!'

Hundreds of feet down from our usual picnic place among the heather the sea swirls and eddies, every current clearly visible from our plane-high vantage point. Sometimes when the Padre was persuaded to join us—he hated picnics and always complained of flies and sand in his tea—he would tell us Gaelic tales of the seven tides which meet at the Mull, a constant danger to seafarers.

On an autumn picnic we often see the basking sharks moving down from the Minches to warmer waters, their triangular fins like huge black sails.

Though not savage in themselves, basking sharks can be dangerous. My friend, Duncan Newlands, ex-coxswain of the Campbeltown lifeboat, once told me why. 'Touch a horse or most other animals on the nose,' he said, 'and they'll shy back. Touch a pig on the nose and he'll breenge at you. The shark is like a pig. As soon as his snout touches anything—the hull of a boat, for example—he lunges straight ahead.'

Duncan has seen basking-sharks go tearing through valuable ring-nets. He has seen one leap fifteen feet out of the water and land on the deck of a fishing-skiff. The gun'les were stove in and for a few seconds, before the shark slithered back into the sea, it looked as if the skiff might capsize.

Before World War II three line fishermen from Carradale in Kintyre were drowned when a shark surged up underneath their small boat.

Basking sharks appear in April, in the wake of the herring, and continue to be seen off the Scottish coasts until late autumn. As a rule they move about in small groups; but once, from the Mull, I saw a school of over fifty making their way south.

A shark—or 'sail-fish', as some fishermen call it—can grow to a length of thirty feet and a weight of seven tons. A dead one which came ashore near Campbeltown had a blunt head eight feet across and a ten-foot perpendicular tail. Its colouring is usually grey rather than black, with a cream or white stomach which is sometimes blotched with black patches and old wounds or scars.

One summer evening I had a close-up of a shark, in clear water underneath Duncan Newlands's boat. Wicked little eyes near the end of its snout kept slewing round to see what was going on. Its under-jaw hung down, showing small and slender teeth, and the insides of its mouth shone like white enamel in a bath.

The shark's food is plankton, a collective name for the masses of tiny shrimps which swim near the surface of the sea in warm weather. Plankton is also the food of the herring. When a shark is 'basking' it has no thought of sun-bathing. It is simply feeding on the surface, where the plankton is.

Norwegian fishermen used to hunt basking sharks off Shetland, selling the skins for conversion into leather and processing the livers for oil. It is said their flesh makes good eating, but when I mentioned this to Duncan Newlands he made a wry face: 'Tastes like the wick of a paraffin lamp!' he said.

Before World War II Anthony Watkins, the explorer, founded a private company called Scottish Shark Fisheries Ltd., with a refining plant at Carradale, twenty-five miles north of Southend. At first, in the Firth of Clyde, hand harpoons were used from dinghies operating from a motor-yacht. But after one hair-raising experience, when Watkins and a co-director found themselves being towed out into the Atlantic by a particularly lively shark—and were rescued only in the nick of time by the Campbeltown life-boat —it was decided that a fishing-skiff fitted with a Norwegian harpoon gun was more suitable for the purpose.

The company had one fairly successful season. Then the war put an end to a gallant venture.

A school of basking sharks is a prize exhibit for picnickers at the Mull of Kintyre. Another is the golden eagle. Not long after the war a pair nested in a cranny above the Goings and hatched a healthy brood. Naturalists came from all over Europe with binoculars and cameras, queuing up to get pictures of the nest. The male was a superb sight as he soared above the cliff, keeping watch on his family below.

When Jock was a child, my mother, always full of Gaelic lore, used to tell him that the eagle, being king, was usually accompanied by a small bird acting as valet to his majesty. At the time I was sceptical about this story, though I knew it was also the basis of a Greek legend. But last year, at the Mull, Jean and I saw an eagle planing high above the lighthouse. Flying with him, everywhere he went, was a small bird. Even with binoculars we failed to identify its species; and though since then I have questioned a number of ornithologists on the subject none of them has been able to give a satisfactory answer.

Can any expert tell me what the small bird is likely to have been?

I used to be sceptical, too, about the country art of 'dowsing', which is the ancient word, origin unknown, for water-divining. Having seen a local dowser in action I am not so sure.

A farmer friend of mine decided to summer his shorthorn crosses on a high hillside. He was anxious, however, in case they might lack drinking water, because the only obvious source of supply was a shallow ditch running diagonally across the hill, and this was liable to run dry if a week passed without rain. So he sent for Laurie McIntyre, the water-diviner.

First of all, Laurie donned rubber boots, to ensure, according to the experts, that the necessary magnetism was insulated within his body. Next he covered his forearms with thick towels, tying them on with binder twine, for it is a tenet of the dowser that the forearms may be rendered insensitive if exposed to the sun. Finally he cut a forked twig from a hazel-tree and tested it for suppleness.

As he led us through the heather and across patches of dry thick grass, he held the twig parallel with the ground. Once or twice the twig quivered, but each time Laurie frowned and shook his head.

Presently the ground sloped away into a depression. We saw Laurie hesitate. Then, to my amazement, his twig twisted down so sharply that some of the bark was torn off. 'Plenty of water here,' he said.

He was right. Twenty feet down they found it, and since that day my friend's heavy brown and white cattle have never gone thirsty.

Some experts believe that water-divining is a faculty owned by everybody, which can be cultivated. Others reckon that only about one in ten people have an inborn talent. Whatever the answer, it seems that practically anything can be used as a divining rod—a forked twig, like Laurie's, a length of galvanised wire bent into a U-shape or a piece of whalebone.

Recently, having read that one member at least of the British Society of Diviners charges £200 a day for his services, I spent some time testing my own powers. I am sorry to report that my twig remained obdurately dead even when held over the water in St Columba's Well.

Like everybody else in Southend, however, I now pride myself on being an expert on the weather. I have discovered that many of the well-known sayings about the weather are misleading and have no scientific background. 'Rain before seven, sun before eleven' and 'New moon on Saturday, fine for a month' are two examples. 'Red sky at morning, the shepherd's warning' is to some extent true, because a redness at dawn means that the air is heavy with moisture. But a more certain indication of rain—as John Cameron used to remind me—is a dawn-light tinged with green.

I find that the arrival and departure of migrant birds and the re-appearance of hibernating animals can be useful in forecasting weather. The creatures themselves have no powers of prophecy and are not infallible guides—neither, come to think of it, are the experts on television—but they are highly sensitive to minute atmospheric changes. Seagulls are driven inland by the approach of excessive cold. Gnats—and the swallows which prey on them—undoubtedly fly higher in fine weather and lower before rain, a habit which suggests sensitivity to moisture in the atmosphere.

Weather-wise, however, phenomena still occur which puzzle scientists. Admiral Fitzroy's 'storm-glass' is a case in point. Its manufacture is a simple chore.

Take camphor, 2 drachms; saltpetre, $\frac{1}{2}$ drachm; sal-ammoniac, $\frac{1}{2}$ drachm; alcohol, 2oz; distilled water, 2oz. Completely fill a long test-tube with the mixture, then cork it and seal with wax.

The key to its forecasts is equally simple. Fern-like crystals at the top—cold and stormy. Fern-like crystals growing downwards—increasing cold. Fern-like crystals disappear—warm. Crystals throughout liquid—rain coming. Star-like crystals falling—snow or frost. Liquid clear—fine and dry. The crystals form in greatest depth on the side of the tube facing the coming wind.

This storm-glass was invented more than a hundred and fifty years ago by Admiral Fitzroy, commander of the *Beagle* on Darwin's first voyage, and is based on no recognised scientific principle. But it works. Jock and I proved it by making one.

10

The Sporting Life

After the war, it took some time before the ice in my ego began to thaw in the natural warmth of the countryside. Gradually, however, people as well as peace became important.

I was elected to the congregational board of the church. I started to play golf again, and in winter there was 'the Drama'. Peace began to be relative. There is much less of it in country districts than some town-dwellers imagine.

It was the village ladies who, in 1952, persuaded me to write a play for them and produce it. For the next six years the Southend WRI Dramatic Club competed annually at the Scottish Community Drama Association's Festival and enjoyed an encouraging amount of success. In 1957 we elbowed our way to the National Final of the SWRI Anstruther-Gray Trophy, with a play of mine, set in a small-town newspaper office, called *Final Proof*.

The competition was staged in the Arts Guild Theatre in Greenock, surely the happiest and most hospitable place in the country for amateur dramatists with heather in their ears, like us. Harry Douglas awarded the cup to Dunbar WRI, with Southend second. Afterwards we discovered we had lost by only one mark.

That day at Greenock something unexpected happened. Southend being a genuine community, unaccustomed to rigid social barriers, the local WRI had taken it for granted that the Drama Club should employ not only women but also men as players and stage hands. *Final Proof* has a cast of ten, including four men and a boy, and for the Greenock adventure I had recruited about half-a-dozen hefty lads-of-the-village to deal with the furniture and some technical equipment. None of the ladies in the club had raised the slightest objection. In fact, the younger ones were overjoyed by the arrangement.

As we unloaded our props for rehearsal we encountered, coming off stage, the members of a club from the South of Scotland which was entirely female. They goggled at our army of cheerful males and made several remarks, which I pretended not to hear, about the rules having to be changed.

The following year the rules *were* changed, and SWRI teams were restricted to all-women casts. As nobody in Southend, least of all our mothers, wives and sweethearts in the WRI, wanted us to discard our male members, we were forced to change our name to the Dunaverty Players. As such, we have continued to take part in all SCDA Festivals, though the Anstruther-Gray Trophy is now beyond our reach.

Soon after our metamorphosis we were intrigued—and greatly amused—by a newspaper report. It concerned a WRI team forced to cancel a performance of the play, *World Without Men*, because its leading actress had become pregnant.

I believe that for an amateur drama club competition is of vital importance. It puts a sharp edge on the pleasure of performance and keeps artistic standards at a reasonable level. It does away with the 'Why worry? It'll be all right on the night' type of attitude, which is fatal not only in the theatre but also in every other area of human endeavour.

In addition, the advice offered before and during Festivals by SCDA advisors and adjudicators is invaluable to country clubs like ours. Over the years I remember the help and encouragement given us by people like Bill March (now Lord High Secretary of the SCDA), Howard Lockhart, Teddy Horton, Tony Burke Onwin, Harry Douglas, Anton Nelson, David Baxter, Nan Scott and Ida Schuster. Perhaps they failed to make a silk purse out of a sow's ear, but they did their best.

It was mainly due to their efforts that in 1967, with *Out-Patients* by Margaret Wood, we reached the Scottish Final of the SCDA Festival. This was good going for a club recruited from a parish with only 500 inhabitants, and we were thrilled to defeat on the way such famous clubs as the Torch of Glasgow and Paisley Old Grammarians.

But competitions and cups are only the gilt on the solid ginger-bread of the Drama. Rehearsal nights throughout the winter and visits to neighbouring communities to put on 'shows' are the main targets of our enthusiasm.

Most of the Dunaverty Players remember with pleasure a trip to Islay, at the invitation of the Port Ellen Amateur Dramatic Club. On our indented and island-studded coastline the problem of transport for ourselves and our props appeared at first to be formidable. Then our alert business manager, Alf Grumoli, had a brainwave. On the strength of £100 in our bank account he chartered a plane from BEA. Like so many Thorndikes, Gielguds and Guthries we flew from Machrihanish across the narrow sea to Machrie Airport, where buses and lorries were waiting to convey us to Port Ellen.

During our flight we were confronted by a note in Alf's artistic script: 'Passengers leaving the plane while in motion do so at their own risk'. (A week later, flying on business to Glasgow on the same aircraft, I discovered that the note was still there. The pilot told me that for nervous passengers it was the best morale-booster he had ever come across.)

After the show in the Ramsay Memorial Hall, which was packed to capacity, we were entertained by the Port Ellen Club to dinner in the Machrie Hotel. At midnight we sang *Auld Lang Syne* and adjourned with our hosts to dance in the ballroom. At two o'clock in the morning we sang *Auld Lang Syne* again and adjourned to the main lounge for a ceilidh, at which Laphroaig and Islay Mist, great whiskies both, made wonderful singers of us all. At four o'clock we sang *Auld Lang Syne* for the third time and adjourned to the bar near the front door. We got to bed as dawn was breaking.

John McAnally, the artist, then principal art master in Campbeltown Grammar School, was one of our players. Next morning Jean went into his bedroom to wake him up.

'Like some health salts, John?'

'No, no. Just health!'

Dougie McKinnon, now mine host at the Tarbert Hotel, was a member of the Port Ellen Club. (So was Sheila, who is now his wife.) He had stayed with us until the happy end and made a date to meet me at ten o'clock in the morning on the first tee of the Machrie golf course. I staggered out to keep the appointment, not quite convinced that he would. But he did and went round the beautiful, bunker-strewn course in a miraculous 72.   The kind hearts of the Islay folk are matched only by their hard heads.

Whisky apart, however, it is safe to say that only the sturdiest, both physically and mentally, endure the rigours of the Drama in the country. For three or four months the Dunaverty Players attend rehearsals at least twice a week, 'come rain, snow or lightning bolt'. Our numbers include farmers, farm-workers, hotel-keepers, doctors, teachers, housewives, coastguards, shop-keepers, bankers, foresters, school children and old age pensioners. Some of us are forced to travel long distances, with a busy working day behind us and another looming up. We come in cars, on bicycles, on our feet, muffled to the eyes against the frost or sweltering in plastic macs if the rain is coming down. Nothing prevents us from showing up at the hall at the stated time—neither 'flu nor floods, boils nor blizzards—because the absence of one person, even the humblest assistant stage hand, lets the whole side down. At the end of it all, when our words come reasonably pat and moves and grouping show some semblance of a pattern, when our flats and stage furniture are built and gorgeous dresses made out of butter muslin, at the end of it all we appear on the stage and learn what they think of us.

'Wonderful, my dears! You were superb!' (Mother of our leading juvenile.)

'Good, but not *quite* up to last year's standard, darling!' (Member of a rival club.)

'What uncomfortable chairs you've got in this hall!' (Man with haemorrhoids.)

'I wish I'd stayed at home to watch the telly!' (Old lady confiding in deaf companion.)

Why do we do it?

I think, primarily, it is because of an instinctive desire for self-expression. Perhaps also because of the comradeship, the sense of being in a closely knit team, sharing hardships and dangers like soldiers in a war. On another level, I think it is because of the satisfying knowledge of achievement when the applause swells up at the end of a show, when sourer criticism is drowned in a roar of genuine appreciation if an adjudicator sends us forward to a divisional final.

No matter what individual members of an audience may say, the Drama in the country does bring people out from the telly. That in itself is something.

The plays we present are, in general, straightforward and entertaining, though new straightforward and entertaining plays are becoming more and more difficult to find. Because our customers know what to expect they attend our shows in satisfactory numbers, and from this two consequences arise. First, we are able to support ourselves in a material sense and need expend no energy in pursuing grants or subsidies. Second, unlike the purveyors of obscure and so-called experimental plays, we are able to communicate with large groups of ordinary people like ourselves and to present them with ideas which we believe are worth pondering.

I think we are right in our policy of aiming for audience appeal, though, as a result, we are liable to suffer the sneers of the theatrical *avant garde*. The theatre was invented for the benefit of the populace, not for introvert little cliques of precious actors and 'intellectuals'. Of course, not all popular plays are good, and we try to choose only the best. On the other hand, we take comfort from our knowledge that the works of great playwrights are always popular.

One of our troubles in Southend is that our younger players, having been trained to a good standard, are often forced to leave us in order to attend a University or seek new jobs far from home. But we are lucky in that we can generally find recruits willing to undergo the hard disciplines of 'the Drama.'

As a strictly amateur producer I am lucky in that I can depend on the co-operation of a good stage manager. Archie Ferguson, still young and handsome, works as an agricultural salesman, but he can put his hand to any job from carpentry to electronics. For the past twenty years he and I have seen actors and actresses come

and go. We have bullied them at rehearsals and held their tem-
peramental hands before performances. At times we are thrilled
by their genius, at times depressed by their apparent ineptitude.
But we love them all and do our best for them, because we know
that in a theatrical sense the players are the front-line troops, the
Oscar-winners, the people who count.

Archie keeps them firmly in line back-stage. I operate from the
front. They call Archie 'Gorgeous Gussie'. Ever since we did T. M.
Watson's *Bachelors Are Bold*—with Gibbie, the undertaker, talking
continually and intimately about death—they have called me 'The
Grim Reaper'. But there is no personal animosity, no sense of
strain. When discipline has been observed and the work is done
we all relax and enjoy ourselves. And perhaps, as an end product,
there is a small flourish of artistic achievement.

In order to write freshly I believe a professional author must keep
himself physically fit. This is my excuse for a life-long love affair
with golf. (Jean always says I'd rather do without her than the
golf. My reply is that I'm greatly blessed to have them both.)

Dunaverty Golf Club has over a hundred male members and
about fifty ladies. Having played the course regularly for almost
fifty years, I know every bunker and rabbit-scrape in its tortuous
4614 yards. The standard scratch score is 63. Oddly enough,
however, the professional record, held by Eric Brown, is 65. The
amateur record is 62. This was set recently by Sandy Watson, a
son of Old Duncan, the club steward. I think golf, like singing,
must be hereditary. Old Duncan, at the age of 77, can still go
round in his age. Two years ago he celebrated his golden wedding
by handing in a score of 75.

I joined the club when I was 16, when senior members wore
tight 'claw-hammer' jackets and flat caps. Some of them carried
their hickory-shafted clubs tied together with twine and played
with dimpled floater balls called 'Colonels'. Today young lads
invade the clubhouse, talking loudly, while senior members sit
silent in corners. In my young days, juniors who dared to enter
the holy place were ignored by gusty men with beards and large
moustaches. If one of us happened to win a monthly medal nobody

said 'Well done!' He was made to feel guilty of an unspeakable crime.

I remember an elderly farmer, bearded, bristly, a terror on the links, whose nickname, for some unknown reason, was 'Yadi'. One day, with his partner, he drove off from the first tee and stumped down the fairway with his bundle of twine-wrapped clubs balanced on his shoulder like a rifle. A visitor, waiting to play, turned to his caddie.

'Who is the remarkable old gentleman in front?' he asked.

The caddie, a local boy, gave a grunt of disdain. 'That's no' a gentleman!' he replied. 'That's auld Yadi!'

Dunaverty, though short, has tiny, fenced-in greens and fairways which in America would be described as 'short rough'. Cattle and sheep lurk around corners and make rude noises when a player massacres the turf. It is a stern test of accurate, nerveless golf.

To prove the point, it has nourished the game of Isobel Wylie, formerly a Girls' Champion, now a Scottish International, and that of David Galbraith, more than once a British Police Champion. It is also the home ground of Belle Robertson, many times Scottish Champion and probably the finest stroke player in the world of ladies' golf.

Belle and Jock (our son) attended the local school together and swapped marbles and pieces of old clocks on their way home. They began to play golf at about the same time. Belle's father and mother, farming folk and non-golfers, were conned by their daughter into believing that every time she went for a round on Dunaverty she required a new ball. Jock had no hope of playing the same trick on *his* parents.

It should be recorded that Belle and Jock, playing as partners in a mixed foursome competition, once achieved the highest score ever returned for the third hole at Dunaverty. Jock having sliced his drive on to the beach, they found their ball in the moat of a child's sandcastle. Twenty minutes and a sand-pit later they holed out in a monumental 36.

Dunaverty's eighteen-hole course, going out, has the beach on the right. On the right coming in is the river Con. This is why a typical Dunaverty player like myself is inclined to produce a defensive pull—or a quick hook when frustration sets in. During his final year at Campbeltown Grammar School Jock became subject to the high slice which caused so much pain to himself and Belle. He almost suffered from a nervous breakdown before the late Hector Thomson, then professional at Machrihanish, twelve miles away, effected a permanent cure in six lessons.

Hector taught golf until he died, still upright and straight, at the age of 92. Courteous, gentlemanly, but a strict disciplinarian, he was responsible, in part, for the competitive success of both Belle Robertson and Isobel Wylie. Arthur Thomson now reigns in his father's place.

When Jock was small he used to golf with his mother. Sometimes he would come home and complain bitterly: 'She doesn't play in *earnest*, Daddy. All she talks about is what she's going to cook for the dinner!'

As he grew older he and I spent most summer evenings on the course. At first, having a 5 handicap at the time, I was able to beat him easily enough. Then the tide turned. Ever since Hector Thomson put his swing right, he has won most of our desperate battles. In S.L. ('Sam') McKinlay's famous phrase, I have 'grown older and shorter' and my handicap has crept up to 7; and recently, on the putting green, I have contracted Ben Hogan's 'over-60 yips'. As yet, in the pride of his youth and with his name on the Golf Writers' Championship trophy, my son has no such inhibitions.

Both Jean and I were delighted when Jock came home from Cyprus, after completing his National Service with the Argylls, determined to become a sports reporter. Helped by an old acquaintance of mine, A. C. ('Sandy') Trotter, he found a job on the *Scottish Daily Express*, and now, fifteen years later, he roams the country as the paper's golf correspondent. (Earning, incidentally, about twice as much as I do.) I admire his sports writing. It combines expert knowledge with a dramatic human quality which appeals to me.

Like his father and uncles before him, Jock found the job he liked, among people he liked, with some free time for golf, and nobody can ask for more out of life than that. Except, in his bachelor case, perhaps a wife. On Saturday afternoons, playing with Jim McPhee against Boskers and Donald McDiarmid, I listen to them all happily discussing their grandchildren. Sourly I reflect that the only grandchild I possess—so far—is a golf ball.

Jean and I usually attend the Open Championship when it is played in Scotland. Partly this is because we can be with Jock in the evenings, when his 'copy' has been phoned through to the paper and he can take his ease over a drink and dinner. Partly it is because golf, in our opinion, is the best sport to watch. There are no hooligans among the crowds, no screaming obscenities, no fighting when a referee gives a doubtful decision. The competitors act like gentlemen. So do the spectators.

When Tony Jacklin and Lee Trevino were playing the final hole in the 1972 Open at Muirfield, 15,000 spectators, in the stands and on their feet, lined the fairway. Though almost every one of them was rooting for 'our Tony', both men were allowed to play their shots in utter silence; and when Lee Trevino won— God, as he himself remarked, being a Mexican—the applause rolled out in sporting tribute to a foreign champion.

When the day's play is over, Jean and I meet Jock and his fellow members of the Golf Writers' Association, an exclusive group which disdains anything but the highest standards of journalistic conduct. Our talk often hinges on the perennial question, what makes a champion golfer? Physical strength? Physical courage? Certainly he must have these. But what else? What about the moral booster-fuel that sends him rocketing to the stars?

At this point I always refer to my favourite champion, the late Tony Lema: Champagne Tony, the tall American with the lovely swing and the poise and elegance of a dancer.

In July 1964, at St. Andrews, he saw the Old Course for the first time. At the beginning he must have felt afraid, for, as I remember, that week the Old Lady of Fife was windswept and cantankerous, in a fiercely difficult mood. Powermen like Jack Nicklaus and Roberto de Vincenzo fought ruggedly to impress her; and impress her they did, de Vincenzo with a score of 76 at the height of the gale and Nicklaus with a record-equalling 66 in the third round.

But Lema treated her in a different way—quietly, respectfully, with steadfast gallantry. And in the end, the Old Lady being entirely feminine, it was the handsome, stylish Lema who stole her heart.

He stood outside the Royal and Ancient Clubhouse holding the Trophy. 'Last night,' I heard him say, 'I went down on my knees and prayed. And God has been good to me, because now, for the first time, I can call myself a champion.'

He had come a long way from his orphan boyhood in California, from jobs in the shipyards, in the steelworks and the canneries, from spare time work as a caddie to help the family income.

At 20 he decided to try his luck as a golf professional and 'follow the sun'. Life became a gay adventure—too gay, perhaps, for a young man travelling from town to town on the tournament circuit; a young man, moreover, with the warm blood of Portugal stirring in his veins, friendly, kind and sociable by nature.

At first he won few prizes. In his own words, his golf was lousy. But he imagined that social pleasures might compensate in some way for his bad golf.

Then suddenly, as he said himself, he came round to thinking that there must be more to golf—more to life in fact—than 'chasing broads and liquor'. With cool courage he imposed on himself a hard course of self-discipline. To a man of his temperament this couldn't have been easy, and nobody was surprised when occasionally he still panicked in a crisis and was still inclined to live it up as an antidote to failure on the golf course.

But he stuck it out. In 1962 he found himself leading the field after the third round of the Orange County Open in America. Pressmen offered him glasses of beer, but he waved them away. 'If I win tomorrow,' he said, 'we'll drink champagne.'

He did win, after a play-off with Bob Rosburg. He also kept his word about the champagne, and the grateful pressmen christened him Champagne Tony.

In 1963 he married, and marriage brought confidence; not the confidence that comes out of a champagne bottle but the confidence of self-knowledge and self-restraint. He began to take the big prizes, including one of 23,000 dollars at the Cleveland Open early in 1964. But though he didn't know it, the ultimate test of his inward discipline was still to come.

After two rounds of the Open at St Andrews, he was in front by nine strokes from Nicklaus. It looked like a walk-over. But on the morning of the final day the Old Lady of Fife withdrew her smile. He reached the 6th hole two over fours and saw that across at the 12th—on the same huge double green—Nicklaus's scoreboard was showing minus 5 in red chalk, five *under* fours. Seven of Lema's nine strokes had already gone. I watched from a high bank, suffering with him. His glimpse of that board must have twisted a knife in his guts.

But what was his reaction? Panic? A smile and a gay shrug to camouflage despair? None of these. Calmly and faultlessly Champagne Tony played the next five holes in level threes, bringing his score back to three under fours and re-establishing an unassailable lead.

Here was a man who admitted having been born 'on the wrong side of the tracks', but who now showed that his natural style had been buttressed and dignified by patiently acquired self-control. The Old Lady, having tested him, smiled again. She knew a champion when she saw one.

About two years later his private plane crashed, killing himself and his wife. Jock and most of his writing colleagues agree with me that Lema's death drained from golf a little of its grace.

Golf and the Drama are important in my life, as safety-valves. For a few hours they take my mind off the relentless battle with words, and I can return to it refreshed.

I love writing, especially books and radio scripts, but never have I found it easy. Every day I require a full eight hours to reach my target of a thousand words, and the work on them is still not finished.

This book, for example, was composed first in longhand in an exercise book. The longhand was revised, several times. I typed out the resultant mess of hieroglyphics, using two fingers on each hand, following which the typescript was revised again, several times. With five months of solid effort in the background, it was then posted to my typist, Olive Wadsworth, who lives in Portpatrick. She cast a keen Yorkshire eye on it, correcting my spelling and pointing out a number of inconsistencies. Her 'fair copies', when I received them, were thoroughly checked out and eventually forwarded to my publisher looking as if a crazy hen had walked over the immaculate pages. As a final chore my publisher and his assistants did some expert polishing.

Any easy flow discernible in my writing is due not to a natural facility but to grim labour supplemented by valuable secretarial and editorial advice.

I have breathless admiration for my Kintyre colleague and neighbour, W. ('Bill') Murdoch Duncan, who writes twelve novels a year under his own name and five pseudonyms. (John Cassells and Peter Malloch are only two of these.) He completes a 50,000 word thriller in about a week, working each day from six in the morning until midnight. My mind boggles at the thought.

I asked him once how on earth he managed to survive. He studied the tobacco in his favourite pipe, and his broad, weatherbeaten face brightened with an unexpected smile. 'I'm the luckiest author in Britain,' he told me. 'I have a fortnight's holiday every month. I write a book in, say, eight days. The next six days I spend correcting proofs and attending to my mail. When that's done I have a fortnight of freedom until the next book has to be written.'

It sounds simple. Too simple. Bill must have a different kind of brain from mine, cool, clear and disciplined compared with the thing I own—a thing described by Sandy Banks, our old English master, as 'woolly and wobbly'.

After the war, and especially during the 1950s, I wrote hundreds of radio scripts for BBC Children's Hour. Science fiction hadn't then been overtaken by scientific facts like the moon landings and the Martian probes, and my *Lost Planet* stories, first commissioned in Scotland by Kathleen Garscadden ('Auntie Kathleen'), were broadcast in all British regions and subsequently in many other countries. The 'books of the plays' sold well, too. Indeed, they are still selling in such unlikely places as Israel and Japan.

Two *Lost Planet* television serials were produced in London by Kevin Sheldon. Once, when I happened to be in the studios, watching Kevin's cast and cameras in operation, Kathleen joined me. After a while she sighed and shook her head. 'Nothing is left to the imagination, is it? In radio you set a child's imagination to work. Your Lost Planet becomes *his* Lost Planet. In television it's a case of take it or leave it. A child's knowledge may be improved, but his imagination is stunted.'

She had a point.

An old man in my brother Kenneth's congregation was perturbed by my imaginings. 'All this story telling about rockets tae the moon and tae the stars, it's no' right. It's blasphemy!'

'Blasphemy?' said Kenneth, surprised.

'Ay. Naebody'll ever set fit on the moon. Dae ye no' mind what it says in the Bible—"the moon by night thee shall not smite"?'

Years later the same old man was confronted by television pictures of astronauts walking in a lunar crater. He still refused to accept the evidence of his eyes. 'Ach, they're no' true, thae photos! They were taken up some gully!'

In the 1950s I was also busy with an adult radio series called *The Glens of Glendale*. For this, over a period of five years—from 1954 to 1959—I wrote 117 episodes, each lasting 25 minutes. To begin with, my fee for each script was £25. Eventually it rose to £31.

The series was extremely popular, judging by the BBC's listening figures and by the number of letters about it I had to answer; but, as far as I know, it was never mentioned throughout its run by any of the Scottish radio critics. Perhaps they were being kind.

My original idea was that stories based on life in an ordinary Scottish parish, with particular reference to life in an ordinary Scottish manse, might appeal to listeners. I claimed ability to write it because I had been brought up in such a manse and still lived in such a parish. The BBC approved the proposition.

Characters and incidents were drawn from reality. The Rev. P. J. Glen and his wife had traits in common with my father and mother. Grizel, the maid, shared many qualities with Maimie, who looked after our family for almost fifty years. Willie the Bomber, however, was a character created by Jameson Clark and myself; a typical sturdy and independent son of Scotland, subject to more than one human weakness.

Jameson, still a shining star in the BBC firmament, has a great affection for Willie, and this came out in his superb playing of the part. I had—and still have—a great affection for Jameson.

An episode in the early days concerned a poaching expedition by Willie and Sandy, the son of the manse, who lulled their consciences with the argument that because the salmon was to be eaten by a Moderator of the Church of Scotland its capture might be regarded as a holy quest. Many listeners imagined this to be entertaining fiction; but as readers of *Salt in My Porridge* will know, it was based firmly on truth. Like Sandy as he bagged his fish, I, too, fell headlong into the burn. And I remember yet how much the Moderator enjoyed the salmon we caught for him.

The Glens was handled by a number of producers, including James MacTaggart, Finlay J. Macdonald, James Crampsey, A. P. Lee and W. Gordon Smith. But the original 'commanding officer' was David Pat Walker, who is now Head of Programmes in Scotland. To play the Rev. P. J. Glen he chose Alex Allan, a brother of the late Rev. Tom Allan of the Tell Scotland Movement. No choice could have been more appropriate, and Alex's warm, sympathetic but sometimes pardonably irritated voice was heard in every broadcast—a brave record.

Madeleine Christie (David Pat Walker's mother) was the original Mrs Glen. She left us half-way through the series to work in London, and I nearly wept. No one, I thought, could possibly take her place. But Nora Laidlaw stepped in gallantly, and Mrs Glen lived on, as kind and efficient as ever. Effie Morrison was the one and only Grizel, and young Derek Howat, whose voice broke just at the right time, played Sandy.

The names of others included in the cast read like a Scottish actors' roll of honour: Lousie Maclaren, David Mowat, Hilda Case and her husband Douglas Robin, Iain Cuthbertson, Michael Elder, Neil Brown, Meg Buchanan, Paul Curran, Hilary Thomson, Bryden Murdoch, Celia Struthers, Joyce Bain. And Jimmy Sutherland, who now guides my halting speech when Bill Tennant interviews me on STV.

Though it had many friends, *The Glens* also had detractors. This was because some of the characters used swear-words, drank heavily and had illegitimate children. In a parish like Glendale, however, swearing, drink and illegitimate children, like births, deaths and marriages, are all part of the picture, and our aim was

to portray warm human values against this background. There is
cause for reflection in what the late Rev. Kenneth MacLeod of
Gigha used to say: 'I'm always suspicious of a man who never
smokes or drinks or goes with girls—and who likes cocoa!'

I believe in the parish, in country or in town, as a breeding-
ground for sturdy individualism. That is why I love 'Glendale' and
the people in it. Nowadays in the world at large, statistics and the
dead hand of sophistication seem to be valued more than character.
Pride in one's own parish—and, as a corollary, pride in one's own
identity as a human being—is liable to be stifled by the constant
propaganda that no one is important except as a citizen of 'the
country as a whole'. In *The Glens* we tried to show that it is
impossible to be a good citizen of 'the country as a whole'—or even
of Europe and the world—without first being a good citizen of the
parish.

When the Rev. P. J. Glen made a New Year resolution and
decided to build a hen-house, neither statistics nor sophistication
played a part in the neighbours' response to his feeble cries for
help.

Many times, after *The Glens* went off the air in 1959, the suggestion was made that the series should be translated into television.
It was never taken seriously, however, until David Pat Walker
returned to the BBC in Glasgow after a spell in Northern Ireland.

One day, two years ago, he and I met by appointment at Cairn-
baan, near Lochgilphead in Argyll, like Cameron of Lochiel and
the Young Pretender before Culloden. We discussed the idea once
again, and I went home to write a trial script. That weekend the
news that ITV (Granada) was going ahead with a series based on
the life of a Scottish country minister, *Adam Smith, DD*, was
published in most newspapers. As a result, *The Glens*, in television
terms, was killed stone dead.

To me it was a bitter disappointment. To have seen, in the flesh,
Jameson Clark as Willie the Bomber and Effie Morrison as Grizel,
would have given me—and, I think, many other people, a load of
pleasure.

But before this unexpected disaster took place I had become
involved with BBC television in other exciting ploys.

11

The Tale of the Happy Golfer

The Rev. Ronald Falconer, DD, OBE, was with the BBC from 1945 until his retirement in 1971.

When he and I first met he had made Religious Broadcasting in Scotland the best in the world. People from Australia, New Zealand, Ghana, Uganda, Kenya, India and Germany all came to train under him at Broadcasting House in Glasgow. He was the 'onlie begetter' of the programme *Songs of Praise*, which was adopted by all regions and, indeed, by the broadcasting services of many countries abroad.

He scorned the rarified, twee approach to religion and employed to spread the word robust thinkers like Willie Barclay, Hugh Douglas, Campbell MacLean, Jimmy Dow, John R. Gray and Leonard Small, who, each in his own way, spoke for Christianity and Scotland in straightforward and popular terms.

Once, drinking a cup of tea in a café in Byres Road, Glasgow, I was joined at my table by a lady who said she was a cleaner at the Western Infirmary. I steered the conversation towards religious broadcasting. She told me she had been listening to Dr Barclay only two nights before. 'That's a man I can understand. He makes the Bible talk to me. And Mr Dow. There's another who speaks my language.'

Sometimes, when I watch television and am confronted by two or three 'intellectuals'—divine or otherwise—arguing about some narrow, esoteric point of doctrine, I want to shout at them: 'There's an old lady in a café in Glasgow whose soul is just as important as yours. She has a great longing for comfort and truth, but she can't understand a word you're saying. Try to remember *us*, the ordinary sinners. For God's sake!'

Another of my cleaner's favourites was Hugh Douglas. I am also a fan of his, ever since the day, during an official visit to Kintyre, he exchanged his Moderatorial breeches for a pair of flannels and played golf with me at Dunaverty, against Boskers and Donald McDiarmid. We beat our opponents with surprising ease and I gave vent to a few triumphant exclamations. Hugh Douglas smiled, with the wicked twinkle which, for me, always marks the good minister. 'Ah, but you must remember, Angus'—he pointed heavenwards—'you and I have a hot line!'

Ronnie Falconer's first solo production at the BBC was with one camera in an old radio studio. His last personal direction of TV was with eight cameras when the Queen was present at the General Assembly of the Church of Scotland in 1969.

Born in Glasgow in 1911, the son of a minister, he went with his parents to New Zealand in 1919, where he spent nearly ten years of his younger life. At that time his ambition was to be a sheep-farmer; but when the family returned to Scotland in 1928 he chose to become a minister instead and eventually graduated BD at Aberdeen University. For two years he was assistant at St Machar's Cathedral, Aberdeen, before being inducted to Trinity Parish Church in Coatdyke.

Ronnie would have made a good sheep farmer. It is also significant that in his college days his main interests were Rugby football and shooting. I think the swashbuckling, determined qualities required for such pursuits were of great advantage in his chosen profession. The sight (and sound) of him directing a studio or outside broadcast was impressive. The thunder of the desperate battles he waged within the BBC for his beloved religious programmes was even more impressive.

And yet I have seen this formidable, tough man break down in tears after an unexpectedly moving broadcast. I have seen him, too, burst into infectious laughter when somebody made a nonsense of the job in hand, thus tempering the abrasive impact of his rule. Like Columba, he is 'a big man but humble'.

He once told me: 'I look upon my job in Religious Broadcasting as an extension of the full parish ministry, to advance Christ's kingdom amongst unbelievers and all in need.' He did his job well.

His parish was Scotland. His influence was felt in every part of it, and far beyond.

Ronnie and his wife, Bet, used to come to Southend for summer holidays. They were—and are—an entirely complementary couple, Bet's gentleness and tolerance offsetting her husband's frequently uncompromising attitudes to religion, politics and life. Jean took to them both immediately—which doesn't always happen when she meets my acquaintances—and this made it easy for Ronnie and me to slip away to the golf course, sometimes with his son, Marshall.

It hit me like a sledgehammer when one day he suggested I should try to do a series of late night television Epilogues. I was aware at once of numerous objections.

I wasn't a minister. I wasn't even a good Christian, because in my life, at one time or another, I have broken most of the commandments. In such a case, could I be of help to a viewer in need of spirtual comfort? I had a stammer, or at any rate, the stammer that had plagued me in my youth was liable to recur if I became nervous; and if I were confronted by glaring cameras I was going to be nervous, that was for sure.

And yet, in my secret thoughts, I wanted to do the job. Pressing hard against my lack of confidence was the tradition of preaching and teaching which lay behind the family name of MacVicar, son of the vicar. Perhaps I did have something to say, one questioning, doubtful man to other questioning, doubtful men. Perhaps a spark might occur between positive and negative poles, creating a small light among many great ones.

Like a coward I said to Ronnie: 'May I write a series of Epilogues for someone else to read?'

He gave me an old-fashioned look but, surprisingly, agreed.

Watching my scripts being read, I knew at once it was no good. I discovered that words and ideas, if transmitted on television at second-hand, lose much of their impact. If I was going to teach and preach I should have to do it myself. But what if I stammered and stuttered and failed to put across any words at all? What if I did put words across and people found no good in them?

Having said my prayers, I told Ronnie that if he wanted more Epilogues I would speak them in person. He smiled, in his usual knowledgeable way. 'I thought you'd come round to it,' he said. Under his breath he may have added the old Scots proverb: 'There are more ways of coaxing a horse to the water than dragging him by the bridle.'

I wrote my five minute pieces. They were about people who had helped me on the way, who had, perhaps, been unaware that they were helping: people like the Dowager Duchess at Macharioch, like Maimie, like old Hugh the kirk treasurer, like the Padre and my mother. Ronnie approved them and set a date, some weeks ahead, for the recording at Broadcasting House in Glasgow.

As the deadline approached I became so nervous that Jean found me hard to live with. It is possible my mental condition was like that of a woman about to have her first baby.

At that time our doctor in Southend was a lady. I went to her and described my symptoms. She was sympathetic but told me that drugs were never much good for this kind of thing. However, if I felt I must have *something* she'd let me have a few tablets, which I believe she called dexamphetamine.

'Take two of these.' she said, 'half-an-hour before you go to the BBC.'

The day of the recording came, and I travelled to Glasgow. Before leaving the hotel I took my two tablets. They had no effect. I felt as desperate as ever.

I became even more desperate when I reached the studio and was kept waiting, for what seemed like a century, while the producer did his line-up of camera positions. Then, in a haze of sweat and incipient tears—caused, I hope, by the hot studio lights—I was sitting at a desk surrounded by a score of people: the producer, his secretary, vision-mixers, studio and floor managers, cameramen, sound men, lighting experts, caption operators, autocue operators and engineers of every description. They were all looking at me, apparently confident that when the time came I should talk naturally and easily. I had forgotten the very meaning of the word 'confident'.

Then the floor manager said, 'All Set?' I said, 'Yes', in a kind of squeak. He turned and surveyed his troops deployed throughout the studio. 'In thirty seconds from now,' he said, and the hand of the big clock began to sweep round.

In those thirty seconds I thought of all the lucky people who *weren't* condemned to speak on television—Jean, Jock, my friends playing golf on some beautiful course. 'Oh, God, our help in ages past,' I said to myself.

Out of the blue I remembered a story—the story of a young minister who went as pulpit supply to a Lowland parish, many years ago. It was his first church service, and he was exceedingly nervous. He managed to plough a lonely, rocky way until it was time for the sermon. 'My—text this m-morning is from St Luke, chapter 15, verse 18, from the—from the story of the p-prodigal son: 'I will arise and g-go to my father'.'' As he uttered the words terror made his mind a complete blank. " 'I will arise and g-go to my father'," he repeated. No light or courage came. " 'I will arise and g-go to my father'," he gibbered again. His mind remained a blank. At this point panic seized him. He girded his robes about his middle and fled from the pulpit, down along the aisle to the exit. As he disappeared an old elder sitting in a pew near the door called out: 'Tell yer faither I was asking' for him!'

A cruel story, as I can understand, but it has always made me laugh. And now, as the clock surged on, I saw the funny side of my own predicament. Suddenly I was less tense.

A red light came up on the camera in front, the floor manager signalled me with a sweep of his arm. I was off, on my own, aware of the autocue moving round, but with the feeling that I was talking to a particular friend in a small room.

It took about an hour and a half to record the five talks. In the process I succumbed to a stammer only once, and the producer said afterwards it had sounded perfectly natural. I tried to appear blasé, an experienced professional. But I went back to my hotel convinced I was a scarecrow that had been soaked in the rain and then thoroughly squeezed out.

In all, I did about two hundred individual talks for Ronnie. He seemed to think they were worth while, and, indeed, many people wrote to say they had found them of benefit. I am grateful to Ronnie for allowing me, as they say, to 'do my thing'. I am grateful also to many kindly producers and to the men and women in the studio who were always considerate to an awkward big man with heather in his ears.

A. P. ('Archie') Lee, producer of BBC documentaries, once gave me valuable advice on the subject of speaking on television. 'Just before the red light comes on compose yourself, take a deep breath and try to look alert and interested.' In my first Epilogue, as he pointed out, I had been revealed looking like a dead fish.

I am still nervous before a broadcast but have never again taken dexamphetamine. In a way I now enjoy appearing before the cameras. This, I suppose, merely exemplifies once again the vanity of the teaching, preaching MacVicars.

When the Epilogues were discontinued—I suspect because statisticians at the BBC considered them too expensive in terms of time and money—Ronnie employed me several times as a presenter of *Songs of Praise*, encouraging me to write my own scripts. In pursuance of this exercise I skidded in my car over icy roads to Fort William, drove 300 sunlit miles to Elgin and travelled by plane, train and bus to Peterhead (twice).

But of all the *Songs* I took part in the one I enjoyed most was recorded in the Glasgow studio, with the Toad Choir from Greenock. This was a tremendous Scottish occasion, adults and children making my hair stand on end with the quality and fervour of their singing. The fact that at rehearsal I was bawled out by Ronnie for shouting 'as if I were in St Paul's Cathedral' made only a small dent in my delight. (When I become enthusiastic about anything I always have difficulty in keeping my voice down.)

The *Songs*, like boxing, golf and football matches, are, as a rule, the responsibility of an Outside Broadcast Unit and, indeed, provide a great deal of sporting excitement.

This, I think, is as it should be. Religion is a vital part of the hurly-burly of living, bound up inextricably with work, sport and other leisure pursuits. King David danced before the Lord. And, indeed, why shouldn't he have made a song and dance (or, as the Padre would have said, a 'dance and song') about the happiness his religion brought him? David was a violent man, an adulterer, a statesman who was often devious. But in religion he found self-knowledge and self-discipline. And in the end, after repentance, peace.

Peace, however, was usually missing during the preparations for a *Songs of Praise* programme, especially when Ronnie was prowling about like a caged tiger. On one occasion we recorded what we reckoned was a magnificent *Songs* in Peterhead Old Kirk. I wasn't present at Broadcasting House when the news was brought to Ronnie, a few days later, that a careless technician, employed to 'clean' the tape, had 'wiped' it instead and that the programme would have to be done all over again. But I have no doubt he uttered a few well-chosen words and indulged a Walter Mitty fantasy in which he dealt with that technician in a Rugby scrum.

In his role as HRB (Scotland) I admired Ronnie's character and technical skill. Most of all I admired his total dedication to the faith of his fathers. I think he still fancies himself as a diplomat and man of affairs, but of course he isn't—and wasn't. Dealing with the BBC and the committees of the Church he was an awkward, uncompromising customer, and Scotland, in terms of Religious Broadcasting, was all the better for it. Since he retired the power and the glory seem to have departed.

A colleague of Ronnie's at the BBC was the Rev. Stanley Pritchard. I had admired Stanley's work in Children's Hour years before; but the first time I encountered him in person was when he produced a series of my Epilogues. I entered the studio in Glasgow to find a large man standing in the middle of the floor surrounded by cables and cameras, lights and bustling staff. Wearing a pullover and a large purple tie, he was leaning on an umbrella.

'Ah, Angus MacVicar!' he cried, in a genial burr.

As I shook his hand I couldn't help answering: 'Dr Livingstone, I presume?'

Stanley was a pioneer of fund-raising through the medium of radio and television. For more than a quarter of a century he served as BBC Appeals Organiser, enlisting as his unpaid helpers people like Dame Anna Neagle, Cliff Richard, Joyce Grenfell, Val Doonican, Judi Dench and Malcolm Muggeridge, among a thousand others.

Up to date he has 'organised' some £40,000,000 for charity. As he works now, happily, as parish minister in the Stevenson Memorial Church, Glasgow, this knowledge, in itself, must surely seem to him an even greater reward than his election to office in the Order of St John of Jerusalem.

His care is always for others. He is still a Trustee of the Barbirolli Memorial Fund, a council member of the Malcolm Sargeant Cancer Fund for Children and of the Cystic Fibrosis Research Trust. Not long ago he became chairman of 'Action for Disaster', which he sees as a cradle for a necessary and urgent national fund for Scotland. And yet he is no impeccable do-gooder. Humanity shines through in an occasional burst of flamboyance, in a dramatic style of preaching, in his enthusiasm for good food, good drink and good company and, above all, in a rumbustious sense of humour.

On St John's Day in June, 1972, he preached in St Paul's Cathedral. His story of what happened to him, a Church of Scotland minister in an alien physical environment, is a traffic-stopper. 'They covered me with an enormous cope of gold and purple, which really stood on its own feet. Indeed, when I knelt in the prayer-stall my head disappeared right into it. During the long procession, as we halted to await the arrival of the Lord Mayor's procession, the blessed thing stood on its own all round me, and I thought I would never get it started again.' (An idea for Dave Allen?)

While working for the BBC, Stanley and his boss, Ronnie Falconer, were a powerful pair, utterly different in personality but with at least three important characteristics in common. Being originals, both were incapable of wielding rubber stamps. Both saw a goal and went for it, like bulls at a gate. Both had—and will always have—stubborn, unswerving faith.

What is the state of BBC Religious Broadcasting in Scotland today? I believe it is being attacked by the fifth columnists who are also attacking the church.

The enemy's armoury includes drinks and drugs and permissive sex. But these are old weapons, common since the dawn of time, and the church, in its vast experience, is well equipped—or ought to be well equipped—to deal with them. The Padre knew more about drink, drugs and sex than anybody, except, perhaps, my mother. I have complete faith in the ability of the Church to cope with attacks on this level, tragic though the results may be at times, provided ministers and their lay helpers refuse to emulate Pilate and wash their hands of ugliness.

The enemy's main weapon is far more insidious. It is, I believe, the continuous propaganda which implies (a) that the church is outmoded, of only marginal interest to people of superior intelligence; (b) that Christianity, with its frank and honest rules of conduct, is incompatible with freedom and (c) that the family unit is no longer of importance, that young people have a right to ignore family discipline and 'do their own thing'.

This propaganda can be found everywhere, in books, on the stage, in films, on television. It is fashionable today—though not quite so fashionable as it was—to have a so-called 'liberal' outlook. Consequently, many of those appointed to responsible posts in the media are of this persuasion, scared out of their sensitive hides to swim against what they imagine is a tide of youthful 'liberalism'.

When the fifth columnists appear on the 'goggle-box' they are not always easy to recognise. Some wear business suits. Some even wear dog-collars. But the majority are somewhat elderly men and women pathetically trying to appear young by sporting mod gear and curious hair styles and sneering loftily at any mention of the word Christianity. They are sad sights. They are also sadly out of touch with the great majority of their viewers and listeners, because, even from a professional point of view, they are running straight off course.

Among films produced in the last decade, for example, which were the most successful, artistically and financially? Not the silly, though generally harmless horror comics, not the boring products of Andy Warhol or the bleak obscenities of *Last Tango in Paris*. They were, in fact, films like *Love Story* and *The Poseidon Adventure* which featured neither sex nor sadism, pot nor prurience, but were simply good stories with a beginning, a middle and an end; stories based on the age-old Christian standards of kindness, tolerance and temperance in its widest sense, which, after all, are the foundation stones of human happiness.

The so called 'trendy' intellectuals take pleasure in denigrating Christianity, the Church and the family. They also keep on asking 'What's gone wrong with the film industry? What's gone wrong with the stage?' I should like to tell them. Ordinary folk are getting sick and tired of the 'liberalism' and permissiveness they portray. Ordinary folk are beginning to realise that the selfish and anti-social philosophy of doing one's own thing can only lead to dreadful misery and loneliness.

Some of us are afraid to say all this too loudly, in case we are considered old-fashioned, 'old squares', though I'm glad to notice that every day more and more people are saying it, even people outside the church. The propagandists take advantage of our fears, finding in our timidity and slavish obeisances to fashionable thought wide chinks in our armour. And meanwhile, on other fronts, the battle sways against the Christians, because a vision of freedom which panders to selfishness and greed is always attractive.

Has it been noticed, I wonder, within recent years, how the quantity and quality of BBC religious programmes in Scotland have gradually and almost imperceptibly declined? Religious programmes are still there, but in my opinion many of them emanate from curious quarters and constitute an affront to Christian—and Scottish—standards of life. Can it be that the financial budget for Scottish Religious Broadcasting has been deliberately cut? Here is another propaganda weapon which may be taking us unaware.

What can committed Christians do, therefore, to increase their defences? First of all they can speak out, loud and clear, in favour of the Ten Commandments. Modes and manners may change, and frail human beings can never be perfect; but the immutable standards are there for all to read and understand. Secondly, they can demonstrate in their own lives that the meaning of the word 'love', as offered in the New Testament, is care and consideration for others, not 'doing one's own thing'. And thirdly, aware that the tensions and strains of modern living, erupting occasionally into violence and drug-taking, often stem from a lack of faith in the family unit, leading to a similar lack of faith in the country as a whole, they can, by their example, bring about a resurgence of this faith and prove by means of discipline and love that the family unit is a principal source of strength and happiness in any community.

The gospel of reverence for our fellow men and respect for the family unit can blunt the weapons of any propagandist. So, I believe, can a touch of humour.

When ecumenical arguments fly like hailstones, and the chief end of man is shrouded—deliberately?—by the bitterness of ancient rivalries, I always remember a story told by Colin McPhee, a member of Dunaverty Players. His father and mine were with the Lovat Scouts in Salonika during World War I. One night Colin's father was on sentry duty outside the officer's mess. Late in the evening, he saw my father and the Roman Catholic padre emerge from the tent. Both, apparently, had dined and wined without finicky inhibitions and were now headed for the latrines, to relieve the wants of nature. They disappeared inside and, after a short pause, Colin's father heard mine saying: 'Isn't it remarkable, Father MacKay? Here we are, a Roman Catholic priest and a Presbyterian minister, both peeing in the same bucket!'

Propaganda will continue against Christianity and against the Church. The in-subject today is pollution of the environment, but this is surely unimportant compared with pollution of the mind. As I grow older, however, and Jean and I reach out for the old age pension, I also grow happier, because experience tells me that in the end the propagandists will be defeated.

Why? I bring forward two witnesses, each of whom can provide a kind of answer.

Jean and I have a great friend. Her name is Sheila Hunter. This year she had her eighty-second birthday. One day a week she has to rest in bed because of a heart condition, but on every other day she is as vigorous as a girl, sparkling with humour, planning and doing things, not for herself but for her family and friends. Everybody is in love with her, but people have to be careful how they show it. She must never be allowed to imagine they are being kind to her just because she's an old woman.

She lost her only son in World War II and her husband not

long afterwards. Members of her family take ill and die, and each time this happens Sheila looks a little more frail, a little more diminished. But she worries nobody by making complaints or by being sad about the tragedies and disappointments in her life. 'All my dear ones are still with me', she often tells us.

She will probably read this and, if I know her, be astonished and even 'black affrontit' because I'm holding her up as an example to all of us who are Scots; a humble, happy lady who determinedly flicks off any chips which land on her shoulder and has thereby discovered the secret of the good life. It is a secret that has nothing to do with money (though Sheila has a lot), or with success in acquiring her rights, but everything to do with the old-fashioned virtues of kindness, tolerance and reverence for the divinity in others.

My second witness is a happy golfer from Oban. His story, recently reported in the newspapers, is well known to me.

With eleven club-mates he came to play a match against a local team on the links at Machrihanish, over the hill from Southend. After the golf a pleasant evening was enjoyed by everyone. Eventually, however, goodbyes had to be said, and at a late hour the Oban team climbed aboard their bus and began the long journey home.

Alas, in the excitement of departure a miscount had taken place. The happy golfer, unnoticed by his friends, was left behind, under a sofa.

Some time after midnight he woke up, alone in an empty clubhouse. At first he was upset. Then his natural resilience asserted itself. Clubs slung on his shoulder, he climbed out through a window and began to walk to Oban, a hundred miles to the north.

The night was dark, and before long he lost his way. Undaunted, he strode on, unaware that he was now entering the huge security complex of the NATO Air Base at Machrihanish. On all sides were eight-foot high barbed wire fences, snarling tracker dogs and eagle-eyed police, but he remained oblivious of such formidable obstacles. The human and canine patrols remained oblivious of him.

Suddenly he saw in front a large vehicle. Exhausted after a long day, he probably thanked his lucky stars that against all the odds he had overtaken the Oban bus. He clambered in, found a seat near the back, deposited his clubs on the floor and settled down to sleep.

Hours later he opened his eyes. The bus was moving, but was it merely the state of his head that caused its engine to sound so rough?

In need of a cigarette, the happy golfer approached the driver and politely asked for a light. Equally polite, the driver handed over his lighter with the remark, 'May I ask who you are, sir?'

The happy golfer was caught unprepared. 'One of the Oban golfers. Isn't this the bus?'

For the pilot and crew of the Hercules aircraft bound for a secret destination in England, the moment was traumatic. Entering the plane, ready for take-off, they had seen the happy golfer asleep at the back, his clubs beside him. Imagining he must be a VIP with official clearance, on his way to play golf with friends in the south, they had decided not to disturb him. Now they knew better. Were they face to face with a hi-jacker, or even an international spy?

The great plane banked round, teetering on one wing. As it roared back towards Machrihanish radio signals buzzed and crackled in the air.

The Hercules landed. The happy golfer's dream was over. Bothered and bewildered, the sound of sharp questions and police sirens echoing in his ears, he was arrested, dragged down the gangway steps, thrust into a Black Maria and eventually clapped into gaol in Campbeltown.

In the end, of course, he was released. Nothing at all happened to him. The whole thing was what Robin Day might have described on television as 'an almighty cock-up'.

But I salute the happy golfer. He proved once again that even in these days of cold business endeavour and callous bureaucracy camouflaged by mind-bending propaganda, not all the King's horses nor all the King's men can defeat the innocent human spirit.

Index